NOVICE

TO

EXPERT

6 STEPS TO LEARN ANYTHING, INCREASE YOUR KNOWLEDGE, AND MASTER NEW SKILLS

Steve "S.J." Scott

DevelopGoodHabits.com

Disclaimer

ISBN: 978-1-946159-00-7

Contents

Your Free Gift

As a way of saying thanks for your purchase, I'm offering a free report that's exclusive to readers of *Novice to Expert*.

In *147 Websites and Apps to Learn Something New*, you'll discover the best tools for building a skill. In this 9,000 word booklet, I've broken down each website, what it teaches, if it's free or paid, and the number of course it includes. If you're interested in becoming an expert, then this report will become your go-to resource

Go here to Grab 147 Websites and Apps To Learn Something New:

www.developgoodhabits.com/expertwebsite

Hyperlinks Included in This Book

The digital version of *Novice to Expert* includes over a hundred hyperlinks to resources and tools that can help you self-educate. But if I included them here, it would have resulted in a clunky reading experience (and also a frustrating one because some websites will change or delete their links in the future).

That's why I've compiled all the websites mentioned in *Novice to Expert* on my blog: www.developgoodhabits.com/expertnotes

If you'd like to learn more about a specific tool or resource, then I recommend checking out this page and bookmarking it for future reference.

What Do You Want To Learn?

Is there a skill you'd like to learn, but you don't know where to begin? Are you struggling to find time for your side projects? Do you often quit in frustration after starting something new?

We all want to grow as people and expand on our existing knowledge. But sometimes it's impossible to stay consistent with a new skill or habit. What could be more frustrating? It's easy to fall into the trap where you focus only on learning and never get around to implementing this information.

If you're like me, you probably have a bucket list of talents you'd like to develop.

Perhaps you want to:

- play the guitar;
- brew your own beer;
- master the art of public speaking;
- start a new business;
- speak a foreign language;
- complete a local half-marathon race.

The problem with these goals is it's hard to know where to get started. Should you hire a coach? Do you hop on Google and follow the instructions from a random website? Or do you read a bunch of books and create your own step-by-step plan?

The interesting thing about learning new skills is they *all* follow the same process—no matter what you're trying to learn.

You start with unconscious incompetence, which is the stage where you don't know *or* care about this skill. Then, if you decide to improve in this area and work at it diligently, you eventually reach the stage of unconscious competence, which is the stage where the skill is internalized. Then you can perform at a mastery level where your actions are second nature.

The challenge here?

Many people don't believe they can teach themselves. We live in an age of abundant information, yet there is a common sentiment that the only way to learn is through a formal educational environment or by hiring an expensive coach.

My contention is that … you can learn anything… *without* spending lots of money… *without* dedicating thousands of hours to the process… and often *without* leaving the comfort of your home.

I believe *anyone* can develop a talent with the right mix of practice, motivation, and coaching. And that's what you'll learn in

Novice to Expert: 6 Steps to Learn Anything, Increase Your Knowledge, and Master New Skills.

The goal of this book is simple. You will discover how to:

- set a goal to learn a new skill;
- fully immerse yourself in this world;
- meet others who share a similar passion;
- identify the "right things" to practice daily;
- master a skill so you can teach others about it.

What you *won't* find is any information about how to dabble in a variety of interests. If you truly want to learn something new, then you need to work at it every day. This means ignoring the "shiny objects" in life and fully committing to the process of self-education.

Hopefully, *Novice to Expert* will become your trusted guide as you add knowledge and skills to your life.

About Me

My name is Steve "S.J." Scott. I run the blog Develop Good Habits, and I'm the author of a series of habit-related titles, all of which are available at HabitBooks.com.

The purpose of my content is to show how *continuous* habit development can lead to a better life. Instead of lecturing you, I provide simple strategies that are easy to use no matter how busy you get during the day.

Growing up, I didn't see the importance of learning because I felt most of the lessons wouldn't matter in the "real world." In fact, I only started to care about self-education after starting my first online business. What I quickly discovered is you can learn anything—*if* you're willing to commit to the process.

In fact, in the past decade, I've taught myself many skills, like building an online business, running marathons, self-publishing, investing, surfing, and parenting.

And the interesting thing?

All these skills were mastered by following this basic process:

- Know the reason why this skill is personally important.
- Commit to total immersion (devote most of your free time to this area).
- Learn everything you can through reading books, listening to podcasts, and talking to others who share a similar passion.
- Take immediate action, make a few mistakes, and figure out what works.
- Keep working at this skill until it's a habit that requires little reinforcement.

Obviously, there's *a lot* more to this process (otherwise, you wouldn't need to read a book on the subject). But what I've come to realize over the years is that every skill can be learned by following a specific sequence. In fact, you can break down the process into six easy-to-implement steps.

To prove how repeatable this process is, I challenged myself to learn a brand-new skill while writing this book. This would be an area where I would start off as a complete novice, and by the time I published this book, I would have some level of expertise.

My decision was to build the skill of "buy and hold" real estate investing. I picked this area because it's something I've always wanted to learn, but I kept putting it off for many years. Now, I don't claim to be a master at this skill (yet), but I did just take an important first step by closing on my first real estate property.

I feel this example shows it's possible to self-educate *and* act on what you learn. So, if you're ready to discover how to build a new skill in your life, then let's go over what we'll cover in this book.

About *Novice to Expert*

As I previously mentioned, you can achieve skill mastery by completing six steps:

1. Identify your preferred learning style.
2. Pick a single skill that you'd like to master.
3. Build the learning habit and surround yourself with quality information.
4. Take action-oriented notes.
5. Create a project around this skill.
6. Deliberately practice this skill every day.

Throughout *Novice to Expert*, you will discover how to work at a skill during your spare time so it doesn't interfere with your busy life. The trick here is to self-educate and implement these ideas during those small pockets of time that happen throughout the day.

Furthermore, you'll discover many real-world examples for each of these steps. I'll talk about the lessons I learned from building a self-publishing business and from running marathons, which are areas where

I've achieved a certain level of mastery. But I will *also* talk about my experiences as I attempt to learn the new skill of real estate investing. You can follow along as I share the resources and strategies that I'm currently using to build expertise in this area.

IMPORTANT: I do *not* recommend using this book as an introduction to real estate investing. I've included my actions as an *example* of how I go about learning a new skill, but I'm sure that I've made a bunch of mistakes while learning the ropes. So, if you are interested in real estate investing, I recommend checking out the resources that I'll mention in Step #3, instead of attempting *anything* that I describe from my own journey.

Finally, at the end of each chapter, there are a series of exercises you can use to implement each of the important concepts. It's my opinion that the best way to learn something new is to simply do it, make some mistakes, and then course correct along the way. That's why I urge you to read the steps once or twice and then complete the recommended exercises.

About the Terminology Used

Throughout this book, you'll see me use words like "skill," "talent," "expertise," "self-educate," or "knowledge" to describe the process of learning something new. The reason I switched up the terminology is because this book would be a very grueling read if you saw the word "skill" in every paragraph. To keep it simple, please assume that all these terms mean the same thing.

About the Types of Skills

I feel it's also important to create a distinction between two types of skills: repetition-based skills and knowledge-based skills. Each requires a different approach.

Repetition-based skills don't require a large amount of self-education. In other words, reading ten books on this subject won't help you achieve mastery. Instead, the bulk of your time is focused on *deliberate practice*, which is a concept that we'll cover in Step #6. Sure, education is important, but getting out there and practicing these activities is a better use of your time. Examples of repetition-based skills include shooting a basketball, practicing a musical instrument, or learning a language.

Knowledge-based skills rely on a combination of self-education and practical, real-world experience. You'll want to focus on learning through books, podcasts, videos, and talking to experts, but you'll also want to spend an increasing amount of time applying what you've learned. Examples of knowledge-based skills include investing, home brewing, or running a business.

Well, that's it for the introduction. We'll kick things off by going over a few fundamental concepts related to the learning habit, and then we'll get started with the first step of the process.

How Do You Master a Skill?

Here's a question you might be pondering: When can you consider yourself a "master" of a skill?

Is it when you're comfortable teaching it to others? Or do you have to wait until you're recognized across the world as *the* go-to person on this subject?

This is a hard question to answer because there are conflicting opinions regarding when a person is truly considered to be a master of their craft.

In his book *Outliers*, Malcolm Gladwell highlights many people who gained expertise because they had the right combination of being in a perfect environment and having the opportunity to practice their craft for thousands of hours.

In fact, Gladwell popularized the 10,000-Hour Rule, first discussed by university professor K. Anders Ericsson, who found that it takes ten thousand hours for a person to achieve mastery in any field.

So, let's do the math: ten thousand hours equal twenty hours *every week* for the next ten years.

This means that if you want to build a computer empire like Bill Gates, shoot a basketball like LeBron James, or record a timeless album like The Beatles, then you will need to dedicate the next decade to this single activity.

Sounds daunting, doesn't it?

Now, if you're like me, then you probably don't have a spare 20 hours every week to focus on something new.

On other hand, Tim Ferriss makes a great point about skill acquisition in his book, *The 4-Hour Chef*. His argument is that you *shouldn't* focus on how the top 0.01% of the world mastered their skill. Usually, they gained their expertise through a perfect combination of hard work, the right environment, and oftentimes a few lucky breaks along the way.

Ferriss makes the argument that it's better to closely examine the people who started with little or no talent but still reached the top 5% in their area of expertise. Put simply, you can learn more from someone who self-educated and implemented what they learned to master this area—*someone who went from novice to expert.*

For instance, let's say you want to beat your friend at your next local 5K race. Instead of studying the workout routines of Mo Farah (a four-time Olympic gold medal winner), it's better to learn from someone who started out as a beginner, but successfully trained herself to consistently win her age group. This woman is a better source of information because she can clearly articulate the specific steps she took to improve her results.

As you can see, there are two conflicting viewpoints about what it takes to be a master of your craft. While I think the 10,000-Hour Rule is interesting, I don't think it's applicable to the average person. That's why I suggest that you focus on becoming a "5 percenter," someone who starts with little knowledge and then becomes enough of an expert that you can teach it to others.

Hopefully, you'll agree that this sounds like a more doable goal.

So, with that out of the way, let's talk about three concepts that will help you maximize your efforts at mastering a specific skill.

3 Concepts for Mastering New Skills

Before we dive into the how-to portion of the book, I'd like to mention three concepts that will be beneficial in your journey toward skill mastery. If you can understand *and* implement these strategies, then you'll be ahead of the people who fumble around in uncertainty.

CONCEPT #1: FOCUS ON ACCELERATED LEARNING

Accelerated learning is an idea championed by author and life hacker Timothy Ferriss, and it turns self-education on its head.

This concept directly defies many of the notions that people have about self-education. It debunks things like the difficulty for an adult to master an instrument or learn new languages and the amount of time it takes to generally master new skills.

The core concept of accelerated learning is the 80/20 rule (also known as the Pareto principle), which states that 80% of the things we learn come from 20% of our efforts. The key to accelerated learning is to identify that key 20% of any skill and work solely on that section. While this may not make you an expert of the skill, it will make you better than most.

To showcase his ideas on accelerated learning, Tim created a TV show on FX (see it on iTunes) in which he tries his ideas of speedy adult learning in a real-world environment. In this show, Tim challenges himself to learn to play the drums, learn a new language, surf big waves, and do ten other activities that are considered tough skills for adults to master. To make things more difficult, he gives himself only five days to master the skills.

Tim is successful in these endeavors for a few reasons:

- He gets world-class instruction from the very best people in each discipline.
- By talking with true masters, he can define that essential 20 percent of material that will help him become "good enough."
- He creates systems around that essential 20 percent to enable him to learn as much as possible in a condensed, focused block of time.
- He immerses himself in training for his limited amount of time.
- He learns just what he needs to learn and nothing more.

Let's look at the first episode of his show: rock and roll drumming. For this episode, Tim got instruction from Stewart Copeland, former drummer for the Police and one of the best drummers in the business. Stewart taught Tim the basics: how to hold the drumsticks and how to keep a beat.

Tim did not learn how to read sheet music nor any of the other intermediate skills. Instead, he followed the basics by jumping right into learning to play a specific song. For his final "test," he played in a live concert with the rock band Foreigner.

This is the formula Tim used for most of the accelerated learning challenges: master the essential core basics and then jump right into the essential skills.

Now, a case could be made that he doesn't truly master these skills. He just learns enough to get by. But as adults, our time is limited. For many skills, that may be all we want and need—to learn enough to get by.

So, the big lesson when you're learning about a skill is to look for those shortcuts that generate the best results. In fact, when you meet and talk to knowledge experts, ask them for their number one recommended strategy or piece of advice they would give to someone who is just starting out. Odds are if you see the same response repeatedly, then this is a strategy *you* need to focus on.

CONCEPT #2: PRACTICE JUST-IN-TIME LEARNING

A concept related to accelerated learning is something called just-in-time learning.

Put simply, whenever you want to learn something new, you should pay attention to *only* information that can be immediately implemented. This can be a challenge for many of us because we've all been indoctrinated with the idea that we need to sit through hours of lessons in order to learn a concept.

A far better model is to just focus on the next step, implement this information, and then learn about the step after that.

As an example, let's say you want to start a new business. Instead of trying to learn everything that's involved with running a business (like the tax implications, getting a small business loan, or how to set up an LLC), it's better to focus on the *first step* of the process: how to know if a business idea will be profitable. Everything else will be ignored until you're certain that you know the business will work or not.

Don't underestimate the power of just-in-time learning. As you're building a new skill, it's tempting to want to learn everything you can. But if that's all you're doing, then you're not giving yourself the opportunity to go out there and try stuff that will provide practical, hands-on experience.

We'll talk about just-in-time learning in a later section. Until then, keep in mind that it's important to break down every skill into a process where you focus on each step before trying to learn about the next one.

CONCEPT #3: KNOW YOUR LEVEL OF COMPETENCE

Becoming an expert in anything requires you to go through a series of four phases, which are often called the four stages of competence. This is a model created by Noel Burch in 1970 for Gordon Training International as a tool to help people learn new skills efficiently. Here's what this looks like:

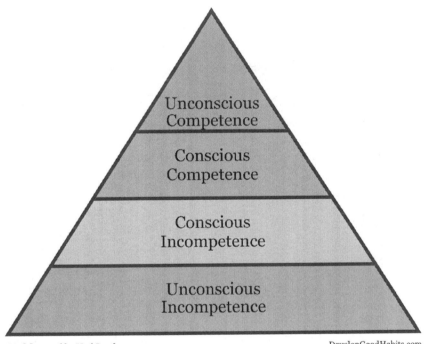

Model created by Noel Burch   DevelopGoodHabits.com

It's important to understand this pyramid because it will help you figure out where you are in the process and how much work is needed to get to the next level.

So, to get started, let's define the four stages of competence.

Stage #1: Unconscious Incompetence

People at this stage are unaware that they lack the skill *or* that the skill exists *or* that they have the desire to work at it. These folks are blissfully ignorant because it doesn't have an immediate benefit in their lives.

Stage #2: Conscious Incompetence

People at this stage know they don't have the skill and are aware that they must work at building it.

This can be a depressing stage, because you realize how bad you are at a skill and how far you must go to get the results you desire. On the other hand, this is also the critical "action" stage. This is where you will make the most improvements when working at this area.

Stage #3: Conscious Competence

People at this stage possess their desired skill, but do it in a very self-aware manner where they analyze each action. With formal training, repeated practice, hands-on experience, and a bit of hard work, people will slowly enter this "expert" level of skill mastery.

The consciously skilled know they are skilled. They realize they are better than most people, but they also need to rely on coaching and practice to maintain this level of success.

Stage #4: Unconscious Competence

People at this stage make a skill seem easy. They don't have to think about it because their actions are second nature.

You become a true master of the skill and can teach it to others easily without needing to think about it. The problem at this stage is complacency. You have mastered the skill, but skills do wither, so you need to work at it regularly to avoid atrophy.

Each Stage is Predictable

The four stages of competency model can be useful in trying to gain your own skills, as well as in teaching others skills. The important thing about this concept is that it shows there are always predictable stages. It is important to know that mastery doesn't come quickly or easily. You need to work through these predictable levels and face the emotional challenges while building your skill set.

Okay, you now understand the key strategies to quickly master a skill, so let's get started with the first step of the process.

Step #1: Identify Your Learning Style

A big challenge you'll face is picking the right format for your self-educational efforts. We all learn in different ways. Some prefer to read, others like video, and many folks enjoy a hands-on approach where they dive right in and learn by making lots of mistakes.

In my opinion, there isn't a "right" way to learn. But the wrong strategy is to ignore your natural strengths by focusing on a multimedia platform where you'll feel bored or disinterested.

There isn't a one-size-fits-all method to learning. Most people have a mix of multimedia preferences. It's a lot like personality types. Nobody is 100% a certain way all the time. Everyone fits somewhere along a spectrum of strengths and weaknesses that may change a little over time or in certain situations.

That's why it's important to have an in-depth understanding of your learning profile. Knowing exactly where you fit on this spectrum can go a long way toward guiding you to the best learning approach for any given skill or situation. And once you've identified your learning style, you should spend your time on just these platforms.

Example

I learned a long time ago that I hate learning in a classroom setting where a teacher drones on for hours at a time. This means I often get distracted when watching an educational video. Usually, when I'm forced to learn through video, I'll feel distracted and tempted to check my phone or status updates on Facebook.

On the other hand, I *love* the written word, such as books or blog posts. I also enjoy podcasts and audiobooks because I can turn "wasted" time into an on-the-go classroom. It's a great feeling knowing that the time spent exercising, driving, and running errands can be fully leveraged into an opportunity to learn something new.

Now, these are *my* personal preferences. You, on the other hand, might learn best while engaging with others or simply trying the new skill on your own. Again, there is no perfect method that works for everyone.

With that in mind, let's talk about the seven learning styles and review the differences between each one.

THE SEVEN LEARNING STYLES (AN OVERVIEW)

Most people are a combination of these seven learning styles:

1. Social (interpersonal)
2. Solitary (intrapersonal)
3. Visual (spatial)
4. Aural (auditory-musical)
5. Verbal (linguistic)
6. Physical (kinesthetic)
7. Logical (mathematical)

(Note: If you're a visual [spatial] learner, you can use this graphic that I've posted to my Pinterest page to follow along with the description.)

Remember, there is *no* bad learning style. There are distinct advantages and disadvantages that work for certain types of people in certain situations. So, my advice is to not agonize over your "type." Furthermore, I urge you to resist the temptation to switch to a learning style that doesn't feel comfortable. Just read the following and then pick the multimedia platform that matches your personal preference.

1. Social (Interpersonal) Learners

- Prefer group-based educational settings
- Process information through discussion
- Grasp concepts based on other people's reactions and perspectives
- Benefit greatly from a positive tutor or teacher

As you might guess from the title, the social learning style works best in groups and thrives on interaction with other people.

These are people that always want to be part of a group and rarely, if ever, want to work on a solo project. They think best when they can share ideas and perspectives with others and see their responses. They tend to remember information better when they have shared it with other people compared to repeating it to themselves.

The best way for them to deepen their knowledge of something is to discuss it. Social learners may not be keenly aware of their own thinking, and they will rely on feedback to refine and structure their ideas.

It's also vital for those with this learning style to have a strong connection and relationship with a mentor, tutor, or teacher. They prefer to be taught rather than trying to assimilate information on their own. If someone with this style is struggling, having them work with a dedicated tutor will help them make a strong connection with the material they're trying to learn.

2. Solitary (Intrapersonal) Learners

- Prefer to study in an isolated setting
- Can process their own thoughts without help
- Benefit from free and open access to lots of material
- Work best uninterrupted

Opposite the social learning style is the solitary style. These are independent thinkers who work better alone than in groups.

They are especially skilled at being aware of their own thinking and processing their own thoughts. They generally do not need or want any other perspective, and they generally do not need to discuss their ideas to refine them. They can go through this process on their own.

This style generally needs less help from teachers or tutors. They are often able to assimilate whatever information they need from resources like books or videos. The best way to help this learning style is to give them easy access to as much information as possible and then give them the time and space they need to work through it.

It can sometimes be difficult to gauge the progress of a solitary learner because so much of what they are doing is going on inside their own head. It's vital that this type be left uninterrupted until they choose to actively seek help. A solitary learner should seek a private and quiet place, such as their own room or office.

It's important for solitary learners to have a clear vision or plan and find the proper motivation. Since this motivation comes from within, it's important for solitary learners to be fully aware of it and remind themselves of it often. This can be as simple as posting reminders, creating a goal chart, or keeping a progress journal.

3. Visual (Spatial) Learners

- Prefer sight and visual representation
- Make use of color, drawings, diagrams, and models
- Benefit from videos and visual presentations

This type is all about pictures, images, and visualization. They communicate ideas by showing them in diagrams and charts. They also tend to need these visual representations to make sense of information.

Visual learners will remember certain things first such as faces, the appearance of objects, colors, and the appearance of maps, but they may forget names of people or places and sounds.

This type of learner must see what they are doing to understand it. They will want to write down the names of people or places they need to remember. They may struggle in a classroom unless the instructor makes extensive use of visual presentations or written notes.

They may also want to take notes as much as possible. Remember, notes don't have to be words. They can just as easily be pictures, models, or graphs.

A visual learner should strive to find videos or other visual representations of a concept. YouTube (and other online video education sites) will probably be their best friend. If forced to use books, they should strive for books with plenty of pictures, diagrams, or other models.

The key strength of this learning type is the ability to create clear pictures and presentations in their heads. They are often able to see the outcome of a situation or project very clearly or imagine what things will look like after changes are made.

4. Aural (Auditory-Musical) Learners

- Prefer to self-educate through hearing and the use of sound
- Benefit greatly from songs, rhymes, and beats
- Like to record discussions, lectures, or lessons to play back
- Enjoy discussing key concepts with others

This learning style prefers sound, music, rhythm, and other auditory stimuli to process information.

Aural learners rely on their ears as opposed to their eyes and will thrive when they can hear the information provided to them. They will probably perform best in a lecture classroom or with a teacher skilled at talking about and describing the information.

They will want to make use of recordings and songs whenever possible. It will be more productive for an aural learner to record a lesson and play it back for themselves multiple times rather than to take written notes or review books. They may also wish to turn information into songs or find such songs, especially when trying to memorize material such as names or dates.

Rhythm and rhyme are very powerful tools for auditory learners. If they put something to a beat or pattern or use a mnemonic rhyming device, this can greatly benefit them.

If they are also social, aural learners may benefit greatly from active discussion and conversation about a topic. If solitary, they may wish to have a self-discussion in which they record themselves talking through information and then play it back. Solitary aural learners may talk to themselves a lot.

5. Verbal (Linguistic) Learners

- Understand information through written or spoken language
- Skilled at reading and processing written information
- Benefit from detailed descriptions
- Use vocabulary understanding as a foundation for concepts

This style is all about words, whether written or spoken. This style tends to align with either the visual or aural style, but not both. It differs from the aural style in that a verbal learner may prefer written words or reading as opposed to listening or talking.

This type of learner will be a skilled reader and will rapidly be able to process written information. They will generally not need any outside help, such as pictures, songs, or discussions, to understand written information. Similarly, they will need this written information and will not remember ideas as clearly from videos or pictures.

A verbal style will probably benefit from taking extensive written notes that they can review later. They tend to love lists and sequences involving letters or words.

Vocabulary will be a powerful foundation for verbal learners. When tackling a new idea, they will want to focus on the meanings of any new words as a starting place for exploring concepts. They will tend to thrive when given written assessments or essay opportunities where they can fully and deeply explore and explain their ideas in linguistic form.

A verbal learner's tendency to prefer written or spoken information depends greatly on where they fall in the visual or aural areas. A strong verbal and aural learner may prefer giving a speech or presentation as opposed to a written essay, for example.

6. Physical (Kinesthetic) Learners

- Understand information through touch, motion, and physical activity
- Need to move around a lot
- Benefit from skits and hands-on approaches
- May benefit greatly from writing and drawing
- May represent abstract ideas with physical representations or bodily movements

These learners have a very strong mind-body connection. Their thinking is often mirrored in their movements, and they must move to think clearly. They have a terrible time being desk-bound, so they are far more likely to be labeled ADD or ADHD, even when they do not have any such disorder. They tend to struggle in formal classroom settings more than the other types, and they may also struggle at jobs that keep them doing desk-based work without frequent breaks.

When forced to do desk-based learning, learners of this style can benefit from having something around them to keep them moving or allowing them to get out some physical energy. This may include sitting on a therapy ball instead of a traditional chair or having a small squishy ball nearby to work with at their desk. These learners often appear physically distracted or restless because they are always moving, but they are more focused this way.

This type of learner assimilates information by touching it, feeling it, and working it with their hands. This can make them especially skilled at sports, crafts such as pottery, or subjects like science that can easily be made hands-on. They tend to have a far more difficult time with abstract ideas, such as those in English and math, which cannot as easily be put into a physical representation.

Any opportunity this type of learner has to get up and move around is beneficial. If they can act out information in a skit or play active games to review, this can greatly help. They may want to stand or walk around when learning. If they are doing something such as reading that requires them to sit and focus, then they will need frequent body breaks to get up and move around.

They may make use of body movements or other physical representations to remember ideas, and they may want to pair various concepts with a physical action. This may look a lot like sign language, where words and concepts are represented by a physical action with the hands or body. This is especially true when learning abstract concepts like new words and vocabulary.

This is a do-it-yourself or hands-on learning type. Simply seeing or hearing descriptions of a concept is not good enough. Physical learners need to perform the actions themselves before they will understand a concept.

A teacher can carefully guide students of this style by giving them short steps and then having them repeat those steps multiple times before moving on.

If working by yourself, try to break information down into short, easy-to-practice steps. Use physical objects you can touch and feel as much as possible. When tackling abstract ideas, try to find or create a physical model or manipulative tool.

Often overlooked, especially if the learner is also visual or linguistic, is the ability to draw or write. These are physical activities. Where simply reading or sitting and listening to information may be torture for physical learners, actively drawing it or writing it down—even if just copying word-for-word from a source—may be engaging and useful.

Paying attention to your body is very important if you are a physical learner. Physical learners are far more sensitive to the feel of their environment than other learners. Temperature extremes or uncomfortable chairs or positions will bother them far more. They may also want to take extra steps to stay relaxed and focused, such as yoga or breathing techniques.

7. Logical (Mathematical) Learners

- Understand information in a highly structured and reasoned form
- Like to tinker and work with ideas for longer periods of time
- Benefit greatly from simulations and mental games
- Should try to group, categorize, and organize information
- Benefit greatly by recognizing patterns and relationships in information

This learning style thrives on reasoning, logic, sequence, and predictability. Obviously, logical learners tend to be more skilled with mathematics, but strength in this learning style can really be adapted to any subject once properly understood.

The key to this learning style is reasoning and tinkering. A person who prefers a logical approach wants to understand the how and why of something as opposed to just how to do it. Once they know why it works, they will be far more likely to remember how it works and what to do.

This means a logical learner needs plenty of time to fully investigate and tinker with a concept. Rushing them through many different processes or subjects or brushing only the surface level of concepts is the worst approach.

Equally important is order and structure. These are very ordered and organized learners, and they need this organization to make sense of concepts. This will mean carefully analyzing and grouping information into types and categories. They will need to clearly define all the steps in a process and understand why each step is necessary. Everything they do should be systematic and purposeful. An up-front plan, outline, and goal are vital.

Patterns are a strength for this learning type. If they can see relationships and predictability in concepts, they will learn those concepts much faster and retain them better. If visual, they may want to create diagrams or charts to show the relationships and groupings within a concept.

Mentally stimulating or strategic games are another area of strength for logical learners. This is a learning style that benefits tremendously from simulation and in-depth activities. They will probably be heavily drawn toward electronic sources of these games and activities, such as computers and tablets. If social, they may also enjoy playing these games in groups and with friends.

A key problem these learners often have is overthinking or overanalyzing a problem. They spend all their time thinking and rationalizing but never actually move toward their goal. While logical learners tend to take more time with subjects, it is important to strike this balance between time invested and learning gained.

Refocusing on goals and end value is very important, and logical thinkers can train themselves to be disciplined self-checkers by setting strict, measurable, and timed goals and plans.

How to Identify *Your* Learning Style

Hopefully, you recognized your personal preference from one (or a few) of these learning styles. But if you're still uncertain which one works for you, then you can do one of two things.

First, think back to those moments when you were most engaged with learning something new. Did the teacher explain a concept using graphics or pictures? Were you always bored in class, but loved learning by trying a new skill and making lots of mistakes? Or maybe you prefer listening to great information through an audiobook or podcast?

It's not hard to figure out what works best for you. Just think of those times when you're fully engaged in a subject and when you're completely bored.

The second strategy is to take an online test, like the one provided by the Learning Styles Online website. If you've ever taken a personality test, you will be familiar with this process. This website offers a series of simple questions that only take 30 minutes to answer. The key here is to not overthink your responses. Just pick the first answer that comes to mind and answer as honestly as possible.

In my opinion, I think the first strategy is the most effective, because online tests aren't 100% accurate. Often, they force you to pick a learning style that's *not* your personal preference. You're the only one who knows exactly what works for you, so it's beneficial to think of those times where you were extremely excited about learning something new.

Understanding your individual learning style will have a direct impact on everything you'll learn in this book (specifically, Step #3) because once you have this information, you can tailor the process for immersing yourself in a subject.

For instance, if you know you're an aural learner, then you can focus on self-education through podcasts and audiobooks. But if you find that you're a physical learner, your time is best spent meeting others in person and then immediately implementing what you've learned.

EXERCISE #1: IDENTIFY YOUR LEARNING STYLE

You can quickly determine your learning style by completing three simple steps.

First, review the seven learning styles discussed in this chapter and look for a description that is familiar. Think back to when you were most engaged with a subject. Ask yourself: How was the information presented? You also want to think about those times when you were completely bored. What caused you to feel disinterested in this topic? Be sure to ask questions like these as you go through the seven learning styles:

1. Social (interpersonal)
2. Solitary (intrapersonal)
3. Visual (spatial)
4. Aural (auditory-musical)
5. Verbal (linguistic)
6. Physical (kinesthetic)
7. Logical (mathematical)

Next, narrow down your list to two or three learning styles. As I mentioned before, most people prefer a combination for their self-education.

Finally, if you get stuck or you're not sure about what learning style works best for you, then you can spend 30 minutes taking this survey: www.learning-styles-online.com/inventory.

Step #2: Pick a Skill You'd Like to Master

The next action is easy: pick a single skill that you'd like to master. Notice how I said "single skill," *not* "skills."

The mistake many people make is they try to fix multiple areas of their lives all at once. A better idea? Identify the #1 goal you'd like to accomplish (or something you've always wanted to learn) and then completely immerse yourself in this area. That's the secret to quickly achieving expert status.

With that in mind, there are a few things you should keep in mind as you focus on picking a skill.

UNDERSTAND THE OPPORTUNITY COSTS

"Opportunity cost" is an economics term that describes the specific value you give up when picking an alternative decision. In other words, when you pick one option you often close the door on other choices.

In regard to learning a skill, there are plenty of opportunity costs that you need to consider. This choice means you will:

- invest money that might be used for something else;
- lose quality time that could be spent with friends and family;
- minimize the opportunity to work on another area of your life;
- dedicate your time to a skill that might not pan out.

Before committing to a skill, consider what you'll give up to master this skill. Sure, you might only work at it for 30 minutes each day, but this is time that could be dedicated to something else. So, my advice is to make sure it's *worth* your time.

FIVE QUESTIONS TO ASK YOURSELF

Your choice of a skill is often directly related to an important goal. If you choose to invest 30 or more minutes a day to an activity, it should relate to a goal that enhances your professional or personal life. So, the simplest way to determine what's important to you is to ask a series of five questions:

1. **Is there something you want to learn that will improve your health or physical fitness?**

   Do you want to try a new exercise program that would help you lose weight? Would you like to get better at cooking healthy meals? Are you interested in learning yoga to reduce anxiety or gain more flexibility?

2. **What skill is important for your career development?**

   Do you need to master a new piece of software that will decrease your company's expenditures? Is it important to improve your public speaking ability to get a promotion? Should you become a better networker to expand your career opportunities?

3. **Do you want to pick up a new hobby?**

   Have you always wanted to learn a new language? Do you want to take up gardening to reduce the stress in your life? Are you looking to play a new instrument?

4. **Are you interested in starting a side business?**

   Do you want to create an online business that generates a little bit of extra income? Do you want to get into real estate investing? Are you interested in earning money through sharing-economy tools like Airbnb, Uber, or TaskRabbit?

5. **Do you want to improve your financial situation?**

Is it important to raise your credit score? Are you trying to eliminate your student debt? Would you like to truly understand your personal finances?

I challenge you to closely examine *every* area of your life. You'll probably discover many areas that need improvement. Sure, some skills might only take a few days to master, while others will turn into a daily habit that will take years to conquer. The important thing to keep in mind is to pick a skill that is personally significant.

EIGHT *MORE* QUESTIONS TO ASK YOURSELF

It's equally important to ask questions that will evaluate your personal commitment to this area. That's why I recommend these eight questions:

1. **Do you want to build this skill, or are others pressuring you to work on it?**

   Any goal you set *shouldn't* be based on the desires of someone else. If you're spending time working on a talent that makes another person happy, then it will be increasingly challenging to stick with it—especially when you encounter a difficult obstacle.

2. **Why is it important to you?**

   With any new goal, you should always know your "why" and have a reason for choosing to dedicate your precious time to this activity.

3. **How much time can you dedicate to this activity?**

   Be honest here. If you can only spare twenty minutes a day, then pick something that can be accomplished in this amount of time. In other words, you should reconsider time-consuming goals like learning how to surf, training for a marathon, or starting a day-trading side hustle.

4. **What equipment is required for this activity?**

   As with limited time, you also might have a limited budget. If that's the case, then you should understand the financial investment required to get started with this skill. A simple way to determine this is to Google this phrase: "[skill] equipment for beginners." So, if you want start practicing yoga, you can simply enter the phrase "yoga equipment for beginners." This search will give you a rough estimate of how much money you'll need to spend to get started with a skill.

5. **Do you have enough money?**

   Simply put, can you afford to spend the money on the equipment required for this activity?

6. **Is there an immediate deadline for mastering this skill?**

   Does this skill relate to an important deadline? If so, then you might need to make several sacrifices to hit this time-sensitive goal.

7. **Does this skill relate to your existing value system?**

   The more something is aligned with your personal beliefs, the easier it is to maintain throughout your life.

8. **Do I have the capacity to achieve this goal?**

   You want to set a goal that's doable in the limited time that you have. For instance, if you've never run before, then you shouldn't expect to compete in the Olympics with just a year's training.

There are no right or wrong answers to these questions. Instead, use them to think about what your life will be like when you dedicate time to a daily activity. Honestly, it's better to know ahead of time that you don't have the time, money, or willingness to focus on a skill than to waste months of your life and then quit in frustration.

FOCUS 100 PERCENT ON YOUR SKILL

Early on, my dad taught me the importance of completely focusing on one thing at a time. Instead of dabbling in a variety of interests (like many people d0), he would identify a single thing he wanted to master and then spend the bulk of his free time in self-education.

Usually, he would get started by buying and reading over a dozen books on the subject. I once asked him why he "wasted" money this way. In my opinion, most of these books said the same thing, so I didn't understand why he purchased a bunch instead of focusing on the best book in that particular market.

His response?

"If I can learn *one new thing* from each book, then it's definitely worth the $20 investment."

Good advice, right?

Now, I don't recommend locking yourself in a room for weeks like my dad, but the lesson here is when you want to master a skill, the quickest way to do it is to completely immerse yourself in that world and work at it daily.

We live in an age of infinite opportunities. So, it's easy to fall into the trap where you try to juggle numerous activities. The result is that you'll feel overwhelmed, making little progress with your chosen skill. You'll become a jack-of-all-trades and a master of none.

A great example of full immersion is enrolling in a country-specific language school. In these programs, you're expected to embrace the culture the entire time you're there. You'll spend your days studying the language, speaking it with your classmates, interacting with native speakers, and touring local attractions. By the time you leave, you'll be fluent or have at least achieved a basic level of competence with the language.

How Much Expertise Do You Need?

While the goal of this book is to help you reach the top 5% of any skill, this doesn't mean you *need* to hit this milestone. Instead, it's better to focus on a specific goal that you determine ahead of time and resist the temptation to be perfect.

In other words, you should ask yourself: "Do I want to master this skill, or am I looking for just a little bit of expertise?"

Corbett Barr elaborates on this question on his website Expert Enough: "Success and happiness doesn't require becoming the *world's greatest expert*. It's more effective to become just **expert enough** to accomplish your goals."

Barr also describes expertise as being "on a scale, from 1 to 10. If you're a 3, there are plenty of 1s and 2s out there who you can teach, and probably better than people with more expertise."

The lesson here? When you're interested in building a skill, be honest with yourself about what you'd like to accomplish. If you're happy with basic competence, then don't be afraid to set your expectations to go for a 3 on a scale of 1–10.

To illustrate this concept, let's say you'd like to ski a few times each year. It sounds fun, but you're not willing to devote *all* your free time to mastering it. So, you would set a modest goal—like being able to ski comfortably down the green circle (beginner) trails or blue square (moderate) trails. And, more importantly, you would ignore any black diamond (difficult) trails or double black diamond (expert) trails because they're beyond your current level of mastery. Your goal isn't to be master skier. Instead, you simply want to learn enough to be adequately competent to enjoy this activity.

Hopefully, this shows that it's okay to work at a skill *until* you reach a specific goal. Then you can move on to a new interest or activity.

EXERCISE #2: PICK A SKILL YOU'D LIKE TO MASTER

You can identify the perfect skill for your personal goals by doing the following:

- **Ask five questions to identify an important area of your life:**

  1. Is there something you want to learn that will improve your health or physical fitness?

  2. What skill is important for your career development?

  3. Do you want to pick up a new hobby?

  4. Are you interested in starting a side business?

  5. Do you want to improve your financial situation?

- **Ask eight additional questions to fully understand how much time you can devote to this activity:**

  1. Do you *want* to build this skill or are others pressuring you to work on it?

  2. Why is it important to you?

  3. How much time can you dedicate to this activity?

  4. What equipment is required for this activity?

  5. Do you have enough money?

  6. Is there an immediate deadline for mastering this skill?

  7. Does this skill relate to your existing value system?

  8. Do you have the capacity to achieve this goal?

- **Focus on one skill at a time.** Even if you *love* learning about many different things, try to dedicate the next few weeks (or even the next few months) to focusing on this activity.

- **Pick your desired level of expertise.** Are you looking to build just a level of competence or are you looking to truly master this area?

Step #3: Build the Learning Habit

As we've discussed, the quickest path to skill mastery is to completely focus on this area. This means you'll surround yourself with educational materials like books, podcasts, and videos. Plus, you'll meet people through niche-specific communities, local Meetups, or even working with a coach or mentor. That's what I mean by "total immersion."

For instance, in 2012, I set a goal to achieve success as a self-published author. So, to master this business, I spent my days:

- writing for *at least* two hours;
- scanning through threads from a dozen Facebook groups and forums;
- reading top-rated books on this subject;
- e-mailing experts and asking them questions related to my specific challenges;
- listening (and re-listening) to podcasts while exercising;
- attending the occasional self-publishing conference;

I'll admit this sounds obsessive. But the lesson I've learned is that skill mastery *isn't* a part-time activity. If you want to become part of the top 5%, then you need to treat it like a time-consuming hobby that requires daily effort.

With that in mind, in this step, we'll review six strategies you can use to acquire all the knowledge you'll need to achieve skill mastery. What you'll discover in this section are dozens of websites, tools, and resources for your self-educational efforts. But if you want *additional* resources, then I recommend downloading the *147 Websites and Apps to Learn Something New* report that's part of the **free companion website**.

Before we get started with these strategies, there are four things I want to mention that will help you get the best results from your learning habit:

1. **Some skills *only* require daily practice.** As a reminder, there are two types of skills: knowledge-based skills, which rely on a combination of self-education and practical, real-world experience; and repetition-based skills, which don't require a large amount of self-education. This means if you pick something like running, then you don't need to spend hours each day learning about it. Instead, your focus should be spent *doing* the activity. If you understand the basics, then you can spend your time in deliberate practice, which I cover in Step #6.

2. **Practice just-in-time learning.** The best way to master a skill is to focus on the first challenge, figure out how to overcome it, and then repeat this process for each obstacle. This is called just-in-time learning, because you only need to research information related to the next step in the process. Everything else should be ignored until you're ready to implement these ideas.

3. **Focus on *daily* learning.** There are *a lot* of resources and ideas listed in this section, so you might feel overwhelmed as you go through it. My advice is to check out a few resources (e.g., download a couple of podcasts or check out a handful of books from the library). Then, dedicate a half hour each day to your self-educational efforts.

4. **Embrace your preferred learning style.** Remember, we all have different preferences for how we like to learn. While I love podcasts, you might think they're extremely boring. Keep this in mind as you go through these resources. If you know that watching videos and talking to people is the way you like absorb information, then be sure to focus on these strategies first.

Okay, those are just a few things to keep in mind. Now let's talk about the different resources that can be used to research your skill of choice.

RESOURCE #1: READ TOP-RATED BOOKS

Why do I recommend books first in this list?

Well, it's simple—whenever you talk to a potential coach, mentor, or business partner, you need to know when you're getting good advice and when someone is pulling the wool over your eyes. The best way to gain a basic level of understanding is to crack open a book that is widely recommended by experts in this industry.

There are a few strategies you can use to find these top-rated books, like the ones I mention here.

Google "Best Books on [Skill]"

I'll admit that this is an overly simplistic suggestion. But there are a surprising number of folks who use *only* Amazon to research potential books. Relying on Amazon alone isn't the best strategy, because it ranks a book based on the number of sales it has generated, which is often the result of an algorithm or special promotion that the author is running. In other words, it's hard to find the classic, most-beloved books in any field, unless you're willing to dig through pages of results.

Instead of using Amazon, I recommend Googling the following: "best books on [skill]."

The listings that typically show up are blog posts and articles written by authorities on that topic. What you'll find are the "top 10" or "best 25" lists that review the classic books related to your skill.

Some websites will be a waste of your time, but if you scan through a dozen or more websites, you'll notice that the same books are constantly recommended. *These* are the books you should read!

If you spend 30 minutes searching Google, I guarantee you'll find the best books for any industry.

Go to Your Local Library

There is a magical place where you can read *any* book you want—for free!

It's called a library.

All snarkiness aside, I feel some people spend too much money at bookstores, on Amazon, or on expensive "how-to" programs. Usually, you can get the same information for free by checking out books from your local library.

To quote Matt Damon from *Good Will Hunting* (one of my favorite movies):

"You wasted $150,000 on an education you coulda got for $1.50 in late fees at the public library."

Libraries are stocked with an extensive collection of new and classic books. Sure, there might be a waiting list for the more popular titles, but read something else while you're waiting.

Also, most libraries are part of what's called an interlibrary loan program. So, if a particular library doesn't stock a particular title, you can submit a request to a nearby location and have the book delivered within the week.

For instance, while researching the real estate investing skill, I identified the best books on this subject (through a simple Google search) and then tried to borrow them from my local library. Unfortunately, they didn't have most of these titles in stock. But since it's part of the Bergen County, New Jersey, interlibrary system, I was able to request *all* of them from the dozens of neighboring locations—for free!

The final benefit of libraries is many are starting to embrace the digital platform. Specifically, you can borrow an ebook like you can a physical book. Sure, the technology isn't seamless, like downloading a Kindle book from Amazon, but it's getting better all the time.

Many libraries are part of the OverDrive system. If you're interested in the e-book format, I'd recommend checking out this site first. And if your library isn't listed, then swing by the closest location and talk to the librarian to see if they offer this technology to patrons.

Start with the *For Dummies or Complete Idiot's Guide To* Series

One of the best places to get an overview of a subject is to read a title from the *For Dummies* or *Complete Idiot's Guide To* series. These are a useful starting point because they cover the subject in a simple, easy-to-understand manner. I don't mean this in a negative way. Instead, I think these series do a great job of walking a layperson through a topic and explaining the basic principles. And, more importantly, these books are usually filled with a wealth of resources you can use to get even more self-education.

Check Out the Audiobook Version

While we've talked about the benefit of reading print books and eBooks, it's possible to get the same information through the audiobook format. This is perfect for anyone who lives a busy life and can't set aside time for reading on a consistent basis.

The benefit of listening to an audiobook is you can fill those small (or not so small) pockets of time where you are busy doing a repetitive task that doesn't require a lot of brainpower (like driving, exercising, or running errands.) With audiobooks, you can turn this "lost" time into an educational experience.

Audiobooks can be found where you'd find regular books:

- Your local bookstore
- Your local library (in CD format or digitally through the OverDrive program)
- Amazon (through the Audible program)
- iTunes (through their audiobook program)

We all live increasingly busy lives, so if you feel like you don't have time to read a book, you should consider buying or borrowing the audiobook versions of the top-rated titles that you found in your research.

4 Things to Keep in Mind

The downside to reading is it's a very time-consuming process. You might spend weeks, even months, on this subject and not implement a single strategy. That's why it's important to make sure you only read the books that *directly* relate to the next step you'd like to master. You should keep four things in mind as you're researching potential books:

1. **Look at the print year.** Recently published books are your best bet for getting up-to-date information. If your skill requires current information, then you should only buy or borrow books written in the past five years.

    It's equally important to get a well-rounded education. So, if you have the time, then you should check out the classic books recommended by authorities in this area.

For instance, there a lot of new books on productivity and time management, but whenever someone asks me about my personal favorite, I always recommend *Getting Things Done* by David Allen.

2. **Find relevant information.** There is a lot of variety to skill-specific books. Some cater to the beginner, while others are designed for a person who is already familiar with the subject matter. That's why it is important to check out the table of contents to make sure the content matches your level of experience.

    For instance, let's say you're interested in training for your first triathlon. What you *don't* want are the books that focus on completing an IRONMAN race. Sure, this might seem like common sense, but many people make the mistake of buying or borrowing books that don't match their needs. Then they end up feeling intimidated or overwhelmed by the advice given by the author.

3. **Check out contrary opinions.** I challenge you to expand your reading options. Every skill has a wealth of available information. Sometimes, this information will have conflicting messages. My advice to you is to read as widely as possible because this will expand your existing knowledge. Then, when it's time to act on this information, you'll start to figure out what works best for your situation.

4. **Implement what you've learned.** Reading is a very passive activity. Sure, you're being exposed to new ideas, but you're also not acting on the information. My recommendation is to read books related to the first few steps of the process, then go out and *do* what's suggested. After that, you can go back to reading and learning about the next few steps in the process.

For instance, when I first got started with real estate investing, I didn't worry about advanced topics like investing in commercial real estate, working with hard money lenders, or leveraging a home equity line of credit. Instead, I focused on the steps required to purchase my first investment property. Everything else was ignored because it would be a distraction from my primary goal.

It doesn't matter if you think of yourself as a reader—I think books provide the best opportunity to get a crash course on the recommended strategies for a skill. So, my advice is to read *at least* one or two books on your skill.

Example Books

The simplest way to illustrate the power of books is to list the ones that I've used to build my real estate investing skill. But as a reminder, I'm *not* recommending any of the following. Instead, they are listed here to demonstrate the importance of casting a wide net when you're first learning about a topic.

- *Retire Rich with Real Estate* by Marc Andersen, PhD
- *Rich Dad Poor Dad* by Robert Kiyosaki

- *Entrusted* by David R. York and Andrew L. Howell
- *The Millionaire Real Estate Investor* by Gary Keller, Dave Jenks, and Jay Papasan
- *Profit First* by Mike Michalowicz
- *The Book on Rental Property Investing* by Brandon Turner
- *The Book on Investing in Real Estate with No (and Low) Money Down* by Brandon Turner
- *Tax-Free Wealth* by Tom Wheelwright
- *Getting the Money* by Susan Lassiter-Lyons
- *Building Wealth One House at a Time* by John W. Schaub
- *What Every Real Estate Investor Needs to Know About Cash Flow… And 36 Other Key Financial Measures* by Frank Gallinelli

RESOURCE #2: LISTEN TO PODCASTS

Podcasts are a great tool to leverage activities that can often be mindless, like driving, exercising, or doing chores. Instead of tuning out to music, you can use this time to fill your mind with knowledge related to your skill.

It's not hard to check out podcasts. Simply download the iTunes or Stitcher app to your phone, type the names of the shows listed below in the search bar, and then subscribe to the ones that look interesting. Once subscribed, your phone will get automatic updates whenever a new episode is published.

The thing I like about podcasts is you can turn "wasted" time into an opportunity for self-education. In fact, you can use your daily commute or exercise routine to receive hours of quality information. If you don't have time to read, then podcasts can be a great substitute for the written word.

How to Turn Stitcher Into Your Mobile Education Platform

There are a number of tools you can use to access a podcast, but my suggestion is to use the Stitcher platform. Why? Because Stitcher has a variety of features that help you quickly find the best podcasts, sort them into a playlist, and make sure they're immediately accessible whenever you need to listen to something.

Stitcher uses streaming technology instead of forcing you to download episodes like iTunes. Sure, you can download an episode if you want, but it isn't mandatory for anyone who wants to keep things simple. With streaming technology, you can move from show to show without cluttering your phone with old episodes.

If you decide to use Stitcher, then I recommend five strategies to maximize your podcast listening experience:

1. **Find shows related to *your* needs.** Use the search bar to find matching shows and matching episodes related to your skill. Once you find interesting items, select the "Listen Later" button to add it to your playlist for future reference.

   You should also check out an episode or two from each podcast before committing to it. Every podcaster has their own personal style, and you probably have your own preferences. So, don't be afraid to skip the shows whose style or format you don't like.

2. **Use the "Listen Later" feature.** The "Listen Later" option is useful because it allows you to build a collection of your favorite episodes. My advice is to cast a wide net when first browsing shows. Then, once you find a few you like, add them to your "Favorites Playlist." This means the app will automatically stream old episodes and post new ones as soon as they are released. Personally, I like to use the "Listen Later" feature because it lists my preferred episodes whenever I fire up the Stitcher app.

3. **Create a two-tiered system.** You might feel overwhelmed if you're subscribed to dozens of shows. It's an interesting dynamic—you subscribe to these shows to self-educate, but if you miss a few

weeks, then you feel anxious because you haven't "caught up" yet. That's why I recommend setting up two separate playlists for your shows.

The first playlist includes the can't-miss shows where you check out every episode. The second playlist (which I call the "listen occasionally" list) includes the shows that *sometimes* have interesting content. Most of the episodes aren't directly related to your personal interest, but once in a while there's an episode you should check out.

This two-tiered system might seem like pointless busywork, but I feel it's a good strategy if you want to blanket an entire industry, learn as much as you can, and skip the shows that are a waste of your time.

4. **Listen at 1.5–2.0 times normal speed.** Most podcasts have 10 minutes of useful content surrounded by 20 to 30 minutes of pointless fluff. Sure, it's good to get a backstory, but if you're looking to absorb the most information in the shortest amount of time, then you should consider increasing the playback speed to 1.5–2 times the normal speed.

   I'll admit it takes a few days to feel comfortable listening to audio at this speed. Some people (like me) already talk fast, so some recordings might sound like a bad *Alvin and the Chipmunks* cartoon. Eventually, though, your mind will adapt to the new speed, then you'll increase the amount you can learn every hour.

5. **Take advantage of the skip-ahead feature.** Most podcast apps (like Stitcher) include a button that allows you to skip 30 seconds ahead. I recommend using this for the shows with multiple ads or lengthy introductions. Your time is valuable, so you shouldn't feel guilty if you want to skip ahead to the good stuff.

It's hard to describe this Stitcher setup using words alone. If you're unclear about any step in this process, be sure to **check out the Stitcher walkthrough that I've included in the free companion website**.

My final thought on podcasts: even if reading is your preferred learning style, I urge you to try this technology. It can be a supplementary activity that fills those small pockets of time. In fact, you'd be surprised at how often you're stuck doing an activity that doesn't require much brainpower. If you load up the Stitcher app with dozens of great podcasts, you'll have a mobile university that's available wherever you go.

Example Podcasts

Here is a brief list of the podcasts that I've checked out while gathering information about real estate investing:

- *Bigger Pockets* with Josh Dorkin and Brandon Turner
- *Listen Money Matters* with Andrew Fiebert
- *Investing in Real Estate* with Clayton Morris
- *Real Estate Investing Mastery* with Joe McCall
- *CashFlow Diary* with J. Massey
- *The Rich Dad Radio Show* with Robert Kiyosaki

RESOURCE #3: WATCH VIDEO TUTORIALS

It's impossible to learn some skills through a book or podcast. This is especially true when it comes to physical subjects, like home repair, computer programming, applying makeup, or anything that requires a visual explanation. Fortunately, with video, you can receive a world-class education from the comfort of your home.

The main benefit of video is how the information is broken down into short, actionable pieces of content. You don't need to slog through an entire book or podcast to get useful advice. Instead, you can find a video that focuses on a current challenge and then you can immediately implement the information. That's why video is perfect for anyone who fully embraces the just-in-time learning concept.

There are numerous educational video sites you can choose from, but following are a few that I recommend.

YouTube

It has been said that 500 hours of video are uploaded to YouTube every minute. This means that it's likely you can find a video for anything you want to learn.

Unfortunately, the above statistic doesn't mean there are 500 hours of *quality* videos being uploaded to YouTube. In truth, most of what's on this site is pure garbage or for entertainment purposes only. That's why I recommend these four strategies to find the information most relevant to your skill:

1. **Start with a simple "how-to" search.** Think of the next step you want to learn and then enter it into YouTube. Since there are millions of videos, try to be as specific as possible. So, instead of searching for "vacancy rates," you would enter something like "how to find vacancy rates of an area."

2. **Use the filter feature.** Odds are your search will generate thousands of results. This means you need to use the "Filters" feature to find the videos that best relate to your search request.

   You have a lot of options when it comes to filters. You can sort by upload date, type of video, duration, or special features. My suggestion is to use these filters to find the videos created by actual authorities on the subject: video, channel, playlist, relevance, view count, and rating.

   Each of these parameters will help you discover the videos that people like and that are created by someone who probably has specialized knowledge in this area. For more information on filters, check out the quick tutorial page that YouTube provides.

3. **Stack multiple filters together.** Even when a filter is used, you still might see many videos that aren't relevant to your search request. A simple solution to this is to try multiple filters while searching.

For instance, you can filter the results by choosing "video" and then "view count," which will display video tutorials (not the channels) with the largest number of views.

4. **Check out the "about" page.** A good YouTuber will include a detailed "about" page and welcome video that provides an overview of the channel. From there, you should check out the links they've included to the videos and playlists they've compiled. My recommendation is to stick with someone who publishes a large amount of quality, free information.

Example

While researching the real estate investing world, I quickly realized that a majority of the information was full of hype—mostly talking about get-rich-quick schemes.

This meant I had to create simple criteria for separating the wheat from the chaff—if a YouTuber provided quality, helpful information on an ongoing basis, without asking much in return, then I felt this was a person worth paying attention to.

YouTube should be your first stop when looking for simple how-to videos. But using this site is often like taking a sip from a fire hose. Often, there is *too much* information, so it's hard to separate the quality information from the videos that are a waste of your time.

My recommendation is to use YouTube as a starting point and then go to the other instructional video websites that provide formal lessons and complete courses on your skill, like the ones I discuss in the next few paragraphs.

Lynda, owned by LinkedIn, offers over 5,000 quality tutorials that specialize in industry-specific skills, like software development, design, photography, web development, and business skills.

The primary benefit of Lynda is that each instructor is fully vetted to make sure this person not only knows their subject but also has a background in teaching this information. In addition, the people at Lynda produce a quality video product that students absolutely love.

Lynda features a monthly membership where you can access their entire library. They offer a few levels of payment, so if you're willing to invest in a premium membership, you can access a practice section, take quizzes, and download the videos to your preferred device. This is useful for anyone who is interested in building a skill that requires an extensive amount of deliberate practice.

Udemy is like Lynda because it offers a variety of video courses, but it differs in three ways.

First, Udemy has a larger number of videos. Not only does it have ten times the number of courses that Lynda features but there are also more options when it comes to the types of subjects. Sure, it has lots of technical videos like Lynda, but there are also courses that focus on topics like self-help, health, fitness, music, language, and how to study for an industry-specific test.

Another way Udemy is different (and this one is a biggie) is it doesn't have a high level of quality control like Lynda. Udemy allows anyone to sign up as a content creator. This means some courses will be excellent and others will be not so excellent. You must do a little bit of extra digging to find the best course that matches your personal needs.

The third and final way Udemy is different is they use an à la carte pricing model instead of a monthly fee. There are free courses, and others are in the $20–$50 price range. Thus, you need to shop around and make sure a course is a good investment before hitting the "buy" button.

CreativeLive is another online education platform that focuses on high-quality videos taught by knowledgeable instructors. Like the others, CreativeLive offers a variety of classes on subjects like photography, video production, arts and crafts, and finance. While it doesn't have the extensive catalog Udemy does, odds are you can find a quality course (for a one-time charge) on most subjects.

edX and Coursera offer free or discounted online classes provided by top colleges like Harvard, MIT, UC Berkeley, Johns Hopkins, and Stanford. Here, you can attend the same classes as the nation's top students for free (or at a discounted price).

Also, there are many other websites that offer a free education from popular colleges and universities. These schools are part of what's called the Massive Open Online Course (MOOC) program, where you can get a top-notch education for free. To learn more about these sites (and the different education options), check out the MOOC List.

Want writing tips from James Patterson, acting advice from Dustin Hoffman, or singing lessons from Christina Aguilera? Then sign up on Masterclass, which hires world-famous instructors to teach their courses. These lessons are not necessarily better than anything else on this list, but some folks enjoy learning from popular celebrities.

While most TED Talks aren't instructional in nature, they are a great resource for inspirational and informative ideas. Each talk is relatively short (usually under twenty minutes), so you can expand your thinking by watching a video or two each day.

The possibilities with video-based education are endless. With a little bit of digging and a small investment, you can get the same level of education that others spend tens of thousands of dollars to receive.

Example Videos

As I mentioned before, videos are *not* my preferred method for self-education. If I'm forced to watch a video, I'll often get distracted and end up surfing the Internet while "watching" the video. Really, the only time I'll check out a video is if it demonstrates a technique that can't be explained in words alone.

That said, I did watch a few free videos by the Bigger Pockets brand on their YouTube channel, which I found to be very helpful. Beyond that, I ignored everything else because I found most of the content to be thinly disguised get-rich-quick pitches.

RESOURCE #4: LEARN FROM OTHERS IN PERSON

We've talked about the value of books, podcasts, and videos for self-education, but without a doubt, the best way to learn something new is to go out and talk to people experienced in this topic. Whether you attend a live class taught by experts or you meet with folks who share a mutual interest, there is a lot of value in exchanging ideas and learning the ropes from others who have already achieved what you want to learn.

One of the challenges with learning a skill is *you don't know what you don't know*. In other words, you might be making a mistake with a critical concept. The problem here is if you don't get quality feedback, you'll keep doing it wrong, which can become a roadblock to your long-term success.

For instance, you could read a pile of books on surfing and watch hours of instructional videos, but these lessons can't replace an hour spent with an instructor who can correct your form and provide a critique of what you're doing incorrectly.

There are many places where you can find teachers, mentors, and others who share an interest in your chosen skill. Here are a few places to look:

- Large chain stores often provide free (or low-cost) classes to improve sales and build goodwill toward their brand. As an example, you can attend project-specific classes at Home Depot, outdoor events through REI, crafting courses at Michaels, and pet care classes through PetSmart. To find these classes, just pay attention to the flyers posted on the stores' bulletin boards or ask a salesperson if they offer in-store classes.

- Networking groups provide an excellent opportunity to meet lots of folks interested in this skill. With a networking group, you can attend classes, find a coach, or simply interact with others who love "geeking out" about your passion. The best resource for finding a group in your area is Meetup.com. To get started, simply enter a key word related to your skill and run a search for twenty-five miles within your home. And if you can't find a nearby group, then start one yourself!

- Private coaching can help you master those important first steps. If you want to quickly overcome those initial challenges, you can hire someone to walk you through the process. The benefit here is they can recommend the 80/20 strategies that will help you focus on the most important aspects of a skill. Coaches aren't hard to find. Simply look for flyers in stores that specialize in your skill, talk to folks you've met at a local Meetup, scan through your local newspaper, or check out the "Lessons" section of Craigslist. (If you decide to connect with a tutor or coach via Craigslist, remember to practice good safety precautions, as this site can sometimes attract scammers or other unethical types.)

- Adult education classes are great for getting a 101-level understanding of a topic. You'll find these offered through your local library or college. I'll admit that most of the information taught in these courses is basic, but they are a good starting point if you're completely clueless about a subject and want to learn the fundamentals.

WARNING. Before we move on to the next section, I feel it's important to give a warning about two types of people you'll meet in person while building your knowledge: the armchair quarterback and the scam artist. If you listen to their advice—or even worse, pay them—you could derail your skill-development efforts. So, let's talk about each one and how to identify the warning signs that you're dealing with one of these people.

The armchair quarterback is someone who knows next to nothing about a topic yet feels compelled to give you advice. Sometimes this is a well-intentioned friend or family member, while other times it's someone you meet for the first time who has lots of book knowledge but little practical experience. My advice is to pay attention *only* to the people who meet the following criteria. Is he or she:

- experienced in this industry through their job or side hustle?
- recognized by others as an authority on this subject?
- giving advice that has *your* best interests at heart?
- following this advice in their life?

- teaching this to others, with students getting real-world results?

Advice from an armchair quarterback can be dangerous because it rarely comes from someone who knows the subject. Now, you don't have to be rude if you get unsolicited advice from friends or family members. Just listen to what they have to say and then immediately change the topic to something else.

(Note: There is one exception to this rule, which we'll cover in the final section that covers the six challenges related to learning a skill.)

The scam artist is another person you should avoid at all costs. The truth is some industries are filled with "gurus" who promise to teach you everything they know for the low, low, *low* price of 12 installments of $97 per month.

Usually, you'll find the scam artist in areas that relate to specific challenges that many people struggle to overcome. Their pitch is usually the same—you can make money, lose weight, or get that girl with very little effort on your part. Just pay them a bunch of money and they'll teach you all their "proven" secrets.

Obviously, the goal of the scam artist isn't to help with your challenges. Instead, they care more about lining their pockets with as much of your money as they can get their greedy little hands on.

Now, I'm *not* saying that anyone who sells a "how-to" course is a scam artist. But it's been my experience that gurus who promise massive success with little effort required are usually just trying to rip you off.

My advice to prevent falling prey to a scam artist is simple: when researching a skill, use *all* the resources mentioned in this step. Once you get a feel for this industry, pay attention to the experts who align with your values and goals. Usually, they are the ones who provide great, *free* information. If you feel like you've already received good advice from their free content, then take that next step by investing in their course, seminar, or coaching program.

Example of Learning From Others in Person

Fortunately, there are numerous local Meetup groups related to real estate investing. In fact, many are part of the National Real Estate Investors Association. This meant I could easily find ones that best matched my personal preference.

What really helped was researching this topic ahead of time (by reading, listening to podcasts, and networking with others online). This gave me a clear goal of what type of group I wanted to join and who I wanted to meet. Since I'm only interested in the buy-and-hold strategy, I skipped the groups that focused on flipping houses, wholesaling, or other strategies that would be a distraction.

The lesson here is to research your skill ahead of time, so you can identify the areas where you need help. This will act as a filter for what kind of groups to join or which events to attend.

RESOURCE #5: LEARN FROM OTHERS (VIRTUALLY)

While it's important to attend live, in-person events related to your skill, you can also self-educate from the comfort of your home. In fact, the Internet is full of amazing communities where you can connect with people from all over the world who share a mutual passion for your skill.

Niche-related blogs are a great starting point, because they're usually run by someone with a genuine passion for their chosen topic. Almost *every* industry has a few bloggers who act as filters for what's important to learn and what's not so important. These experts can become your trusted sources that will help you stay on top of this industry as you learn the ropes.

Now, the big downside of reading niche-related blogs is it's hard to be 100 percent certain if a blogger is providing good information or if he is full of hot air.

That's why I recommend the following process to find the best blogs:

- Google "Top [your niche] blogs [current year]." So, if you want to learn about real estate investing, you'd type: "top real estate investing blogs 2016." This will produce a list of search results recommended by authorities in this market.

- Visit the sites that attract your interest, check out their background on their "about" page, and read their top posts. If you find many valuable, free blog posts, then this expert is probably somebody worth paying attention to. From there, you should subscribe to their e-mail list to get more information and check out any resources they recommend.

- When researching a market, I begin by looking at blogs, because they are often the best source of free information about a market. Usually, the best ones will link to the forums, Facebook groups, and podcasts that are worth checking out. This means you can use a blog as a central hub for your self-educational efforts.

Forums and Facebook groups are the water coolers of the 21st century. Simply find a few groups full of passionate people and you'll surround yourself with knowledgeable folks who can give you advice whenever you feel stuck.

Finding a forum or Facebook group isn't that hard:

- If you're looking for a forum, simply Google "top [your niche] forum."

- If you're looking for a Facebook group, simply hop onto Facebook, type in a phrase related to your niche, and scan through the groups that pique your interest.

I'd caution you to pay close attention to the quality of the content posted within each group. If you see a large amount of self-promotion and very little interaction, then it's probably not the right place for you. Instead, look for communities where people ask questions, post helpful content, and help one another with learning everything they can about this topic.

Starting a podcast is an incredible way to network and meet the top people in your industry. Most experts are busy people, so they don't have time to provide individual mentorship. But one way to "get access" to these individuals is to start a podcast and invite them on your show for a short interview.

Why would an expert be interested in your podcast? Well, the main benefit is you give them an opportunity to promote their product, brand, or service to your audience. This means many experts are willing to set aside 15–45 minutes to answer a few questions and provide useful information.

What usually happens after the interview is the expert will have a few minutes to spare. Usually, they are willing to answer a couple of questions related to any of your specific challenges. This means if you end up recording dozens of episodes, you're masterminding with dozens of experts in this market. I'd consider this to be an effective "hack," because you'll quickly learn the most important strategies related to your skill.

For instance, I've recorded a few hundred episodes (as both the interviewer and the interviewee) with individuals who share a passion for personal development and running an online business. While the conversations were great, the real magic happened during the "small talk" before and after the interview. Usually, these discussions are full of great advice and helpful information—all made possible through the power of podcasting.

Now, if you'd like to leverage podcasting to connect with experts, a great way to get maximum results is to focus on the 80/20 rule. Simply ask each person what *they* recommend to get the best results in the shortest amount of time. These are questions like:

- "What was the biggest challenge you overcame and how did you do it?"

- "If you had to start all over, what would you do differently, and why?"

- "If you only had an hour a day to focus on this skill, what would you focus on?"

- "What is your #1 tip for people interested in ___?"
- "What is the best advice you have ever heard about ___?"
- "What activities were the biggest waste of your time?"

These questions are a great way to cut through the noise, because they help you (and your listeners) identify what's truly important for your skill and what can be ignored.

My final piece of advice is to start a podcast *only* if you're truly interested in building a quality show that's full of helpful content. Podcasting is not an easy thing to do on an ongoing basis, so it's not worth the effort if you do it just for selfish reasons. But, if you like providing value to an audience and meeting awesome people, then it's definitely a worthwhile endeavor.

To learn more about this strategy, you should check out the free podcasting tutorial provided by Pat Flynn of the Smart Passive Income website.

Example of Learning From Others Virtually

While there are many virtual communities related to real estate investing, I decided to focus only on the Bigger Pockets forum. My reason was simple: Bigger Pockets consistently provided exceptional, free information through their podcasts, videos, books, and blog posts, so I felt it was a no-brainer to join a community that was also full of knowledge experts.

The big lesson here is you don't always need to join dozens of communities to meet great people. Sometimes, you can find a single go-to destination that contains everything you need, which can act as your filter for your self-educational efforts.

RESOURCE #6: PURCHASE HOW-TO COURSES OR PRODUCTS

Information courses *can* be the ultimate solution, because they often provide a step-by-step blueprint you can use to get started with a skill.

However, there is a specific reason they are mentioned as the last resource of this section. It's my opinion that you can acquire all the knowledge you need for free or on the cheap by leveraging the five strategies we've already discussed. Honestly, the only time you'll need to pay for information is when you're starved for time, you need a little hand-holding for a specific process, or you want to skip ahead in the learning process.

With that in mind, there are three rules to remember when shopping for an information course:

- **Rule #1: Pick step-by-step information courses.** Courses that have an actionable blueprint are great for the busy person who likes to be told what to do. While you can usually find most of this information for free online, there is a benefit to buying a product from someone who can provide shortcuts and lessons learned from their personal experience. A good course will tell you *what* to do, *when* to do it, and *how* to do it.

    Furthermore, many courses offer direct access to the product creator. Here, you'll have an opportunity to ask questions about your specific challenges—and more importantly, get a little bit of mentorship along the way. This is important because knowledge experts often live busy lives, and they can't help everyone. But usually they will set aside time for their customers and students. So basically, with your product purchase you're also purchasing access to their time.

- **Rule #2: Buy courses created by experts who provide great free content.** I'll admit this might seem counterintuitive, but it's been my experience that the best providers of *paid* information are people who provide value with *free* information. Not only does this demonstrate their expertise but it also shows that they are confident enough about the quality of their content that they're willing to give away a lot of stuff.

A quick way to discover a quality information course is to immerse yourself in the free content provided by top podcasts and blogs. If you find that you're getting useful advice for free on a consistent basis, then it's likely that their paid product will be even better.

- **Rule #3: Avoid courses that promise instant success with no effort required.** Yes, it's human nature to want fast results. The problem is there are predators who know that many people fall prey to the promise of instant results. These "gurus" will make lofty claims that can't possibly be true. And usually, the material is filled with low-value and even dangerous information.

  Usually, you can smell a scam from a mile away. They typically have claims like: "Lose fifty pounds in a month *without* dieting!" or "Get the girl of your dreams to fall in love with you with this one weird trick!" or "Make money online effortlessly with our automated, supercharged, cash-generating money machine where the only thing you'll need to do is deposit fat stacks into your checking account!"

I'll let you in on a little secret—these claims are all complete BS.

Sure, many products are filled with valuable, life-changing information. But the ones that will make a difference in your life involve effort on your part that often requires you to take daily action.

Example

When I followed the rules outlined in this section, I discovered *one* resource that consistently published quality, free content—the Bigger Pockets brand. They provide valuable information through their blog, podcast, membership community, and webinars.

I felt that whenever I had a question about a specific concept, I could turn to Bigger Pockets to find the answer somewhere on the site. So, now that I'm starting to *pay* for information, I've made the decision to check out the paid offers from their bookstore and premium membership.

Now, I recognize that this section has turned into a promotion for the Bigger Pockets brand, but there is an important point that I'd like to make through this example: When you first start researching a skill, you'll probably feel overwhelmed by an avalanche of information. After you start to understand this market, you'll identify the people who consistently provide great information. In my opinion, these are the folks that should get your money when you're ready to purchase a course.

EXERCISE #3: BUILD THE LEARNING HABIT

There is an abundance of information in the world. In fact, with a little bit of effort, you can find enough resources to help you master any skill.

If you can commit to learning from a variety of multimedia platforms, it's possible to get *hours* of daily lessons without it eating up too much of your free time. You can self-educate while driving, exercising, running errands, or relaxing at home. All you need to do is commit to building the learning habit.

To get started, I recommend the following six actions to find the best resources for your chosen skill:

1. **Buy or borrow top-rated books.** Start with a Google search to identify the books most recommended by experts in this industry. Then go to Amazon, a local library, or Audible (if you prefer audiobooks) to grab a copy. (I recommend using the interlibrary system because it's convenient *and* free.) If you're not sure where to get started, you can begin with something in the *For Dummies* or *Complete Idiot's Guide To* series.

2. **Listen to multiple podcasts.** Download the Stitcher app, search for niche-specific podcasts, and listen to a few episodes from each one. When you find a few favorites, use Stitcher to organize them into a playlist that is streamed directly into your queue. Listen to these shows during those pockets of time that would normally be wasted (like driving or running errands).

3. **Watch video tutorials if you need a demonstration for a technical or mechanical skill.** Start with YouTube and look for channels that focus on a single topic. If you need additional instructions, sign up for a course on sites like Lynda, Udemy, CreativeLive, Coursera, edX, or Masterclass. Finally, use TED Talks to expand your thinking on what you're learning.

4. **Learn in a real-world setting.** Attend classes provided by chain stores, community colleges, or your local library. If you want to quickly achieve mastery, hire a private coach who can get you past those initial roadblocks and challenges.

5. **Learn online.** Read niche-related blogs and interact with others through forums and Facebook groups. Plus, consider starting a podcast if you want to connect with top authorities in your area of expertise.

6. **Purchase a how-to course.** If you feel stuck or simply want a shortcut to learn as much as possible in a short amount of time, this type of course will jumpstart you.

If you leverage these six types of resources, you can surround yourself with quality information that will provide a top-notch educational experience—*without* spending a lot of your hard-earned money. And since you've (hopefully) made the commitment to singularly focus on this topic, you'll learn at a faster pace than someone who dabbles in this area and fails to take consistent action.

Step #4: Take Actionable Notes

As you self-educate, you will get a lot of valuable advice. The challenge? You will need a good system to record this information—without feeling overwhelmed. That's why it's important to take action-oriented notes that focus on how to implement what you're learning.

Note taking isn't about writing down every fact, figure, or resource. Remember, you probably won't take a test on this subject. Instead, your goal is to focus on just the information that will help you achieve mastery. Your job here is to learn practical knowledge instead of theoretical knowledge.

For instance, as I focus on my real estate investing education, it's more important to focus on the strategies that help me find an ideal investment property instead of finance-related trivia like when President Nixon took the United States currency off the gold standard. (For the record, it was 1971.) Sure, factoids like this can be interesting, but you shouldn't waste valuable self-educational time by majoring in minor details.

So, the goal of this section is simple. I will show you how to take *actionable* notes from what you learned in Step #3.

While the following might *seem* like the technique you used in school to take notes, it's different because nobody will ask you to take a test on this subject. Instead, it's a "life test" where your grade is determined by how well you execute these ideas. Either you master them or you don't.

Now, let's dive into why note taking is a vital part of the process and how to get the most from the information that you're gathering.

WHY IS NOTE TAKING IMPORTANT?

Writing down what you've learned can be beneficial in several ways:

- **It will help you to never forget an important piece of information.** You will always have a copy of every important step of the process, which can be reviewed whenever you need a refresher on the material.

- **It will help you reframe the concepts you've learned from books, podcasts, and videos.** If you put something into your own words, it's easier to understand and then incorporate into your life.

- **It will help you capture key steps that you need to follow.** Many skills require a series of small actions, and if you miss any important step, then you risk failure or making a big mistake. Often, these suggested steps will become part of your personal process that you'll refer to on a regular basis.

- **It will help you solve problems and work through complex topics.** Sometimes, you might not initially understand a concept. But if you write it down and research it later, you'll achieve full comprehension.

- **It will help you visualize a concept with pictures and images.** Often, a topic is best explained by drawing an image.

As mentioned before, it's not necessary to record everything you learn. Instead, focus on the information that will help you implement the most important ideas.

WHAT TOOL SHOULD YOU USE FOR NOTE TAKING?

You have a few options for your note-taking efforts. There is the old-fashioned pen-and-paper approach, or you can type the information using a laptop or tablet, or you can record audio (which will be reviewed later).

In this section, I'll go over all three options and show evidence for why I recommend the pen-and-paper approach.

Laptops or Tablets versus Pen and Paper

Laptops are everywhere. Go to any university and you'll see many students typing notes into their laptops. The reason some folks prefer the typing approach is they can record information faster than they can by hand.

Now, since some people can type faster than they write, you might think it's a *better* method over the pen-and-paper approach. But the truth is typing isn't the best method for taking notes. In fact, there have been many studies that show how the pen-and-paper approach is a superior method.

For instance, it has been found that the strength of the laptop is *also* its weakness. According to Pam A. Mueller of Princeton University, since people type faster than they write, this often causes them to transcribe everything they hear. On the other hand, when people write by hand, they must think critically about the information and make quick decisions about what's important to jot down.

Audio Recording versus Pen and Paper

Recording information gives you the freedom to focus on listening to a lecture and then taking notes later. In theory, this sounds like a great strategy for making sure you never miss a key point. But as with typing, research has shown that taking notes during a lecture is better than creating an audio recording that you'll refer to later. Here are three reasons why:

1. **You risk transcribing *too much* information when given time to write down everything from an audio recording.** This means you're spending more time in the learning phase and not enough time in the deliberate practice phase, which we'll talk about in Step #6.

2. **You're not thinking critically about the information while writing it down.** Instead, you're trying to jot down as much information as possible, which means you're not making those

small (but important) decisions about what information is personally important to you.

3. **You lose the value of the lecture if you don't transcribe the notes within nine hours.** One of the best parts of taking notes during a lecture is you'll often have aha moments when you connect a concept to something in your life. By not recording these thoughts (and the lecture) within the first nine hours, you risk losing out on an important thought.

Overall, the pen-and-paper approach helps you think critically about the information and make instant decisions about what's a crucial thing to remember. With this approach, you can filter out extraneous information, identify key steps, and then use this information to create an action plan that you'll implement in Step #6.

How to Take Notes Using the Cornell Method

There are many note-taking strategies, and each has its own advantages and disadvantages. But I have found the Cornell Method to be the best method for adults who want to focus on self-education.

Why do I recommend the Cornell Method? I like it because you create notes that are easy to scan. This means you can quickly identify an important step and immediately get started.

With the Cornell Method, you divide each page into three sections.

Here's how it looks:

CUES

- Main ideas
- Questions that connect points
- Diagrams
- Prompts to help you study

WHEN:
After class during review

2.5 inches

NOTES

- Record the lecture here
- Use:
  - concise sentences
  - shorthand symbols
  - abbreviations
  - lists
- Skip lots of space between points

WHEN: *During class*

6 inches

SUMMARY

Top level main ideas for quick reference
WHEN: *After class during review*

2 inches

DEVELOPGOODHABITS.COM

You can create your own version of Cornell notes by doing the following three things (if you're using the standard 8 ½-inch by 11-inch lined paper):

1. Draw a horizontal line above the bottom four lines of your paper.

2. Draw a vertical line 2 ½ inches from the left side of your paper down to the pinkish horizontal line that comes standard with most lined paper.

3. Do this for many pages in advance, so you can flip from page to page in your notes without having to worry about setting up your pages.

This creates three separate sections that will be used during an important lesson.

GETTING STARTED WITH THE CORNELL METHOD

Since the Cornell-formatted page is broken down into three sections, let's go over what you'll include in each section.

The largest section is the upper right part of the page. This area will have a six-inch block where you can write down ideas and important information as they're being taught. In this section, you should:

- use concise sentences to record key points;
- pull out key words and main ideas;
- write down anything displayed on a projection slide or written on a board;
- emphasize anything repeated or stressed;
- use shorthand symbols and abbreviations when possible;
- create lists of important steps or strategies; and
- copy diagrams and pictures.

This section is used for your first introduction to the material. It doesn't matter if you're reading a book, sitting through a lecture, or watching a video—this will be the section where you jot down the critical information when you're seeing it for the first time.

The second section will include all the important cues. This is a 2- to 2 ½-inch area on the left side of the page that's reserved for any notes *after* the lesson. This will allow you to review the material and pull out information that's critical to your long-term success.

Also, these cues help you remember lengthy information from the main section without forcing you to reread the entire thing.

You should include these items in the left section:

- Key words
- Main ideas
- Essential questions
- Prompts to help you remember info

The main benefit of the left section is you can review this page in a minute, identify the key points, and avoid having to waste time completely rereading the information if you're simply looking for a reminder about an important concept.

The third section will include the information you write down in the two inches at the bottom of the page. These are the notes you'll create during a follow-up study session. In the bottom section, you need to summarize, in your own words, the *main lesson* that's covered on this page.

The reason you should create a summary in this limited area is because it forces you to think critically about what you have learned, reinforce the knowledge, and identify the concepts that you might not understand that need to be researched further.

Once you have a summary on every page, it will also help later study sessions when you are trying to find a specific piece of information a few weeks (or months) after you first learned it. This is a time-saver, because all you'll need to do is read the summary on each page to find the concept you're looking for.

My Personal Note-Taking Hack

In my opinion, the biggest flaw of the Cornell Method is it assumes a person only learns in a live classroom setting. Since we now know it's possible to self-educate through books, podcasts, videos, and websites, I feel it's important to talk about how to incorporate this technology into your note-taking efforts regardless of your learning style.

I recommend you also jot down the *key markers* from the various multimedia you consume while learning a skill. Just create a summary of the concept discussed and then add a reminder of where to find a full explanation. This is a useful technique for when you don't want to record an entire block of text or copy a wordy diagram. All you need to do is create a reference for this information.

For instance, you can create key markers in your Cornell notes for the following items:

- Templates
- Diagrams
- Worksheets
- Resource sections
- Case studies
- Examples

And a marker can be any of the following:

- Page numbers of a book
- A name of a podcast with the episode number
- Time stamp of a video
- Link to a specific page on a website
- Reminder of any notes uploaded to Evernote

If you choose to add this shortcut to your Cornell note-taking efforts, then you'll save a lot of time because you won't feel the need to write down everything. This is time that can be repurposed for the implement phase of your skill-mastery efforts.

COMPRESS YOUR NOTES INTO A "ONE-PAGER"

In a previous section, I told a brief story about how my dad would approach learning about a new skill—reading a dozen or more books on the subject and taking lots of notes. After going through these books, he would end up with pages of notes, diagrams, and resources on this subject. What he would do after that is a strategy I now use all the time.

Once my dad finished these books, he would go through his pages of notes and condense the information into a few smaller pages. He would then repeat this process again and again—each time reducing the text into a smaller collection of rules and guidelines. Eventually, he would be left with a single page that contained only the most important information related to that skill. He called this his "one-pager."

The advantage of a one-pager is you have a cheat sheet of the specific steps you need to take to master this skill. It includes the repetitive actions to do daily (i.e., habits) *and* the single actions to complete. In a way, this one-pager acts as a recipe that shows how to succeed with a skill.

To illustrate the one-pager concept, let me talk about how I compressed all I know about self-publishing into a single document.

In 2012, I knew nothing about the self-publishing business model. But after an intensive amount of learning (and implementation), I eventually created a series of rules and guidelines that I consider to be an important part of the publishing process. Eventually, these notes turned into a simple list with over 50 steps that I follow whenever I start a new book project. All I have to do is pull out this list and follow each step of the process. (You can even see an example of this one-pager in the free companion website.)

You don't need pages of notes to master a skill. Instead, once you can identify the critical 80/20 strategies, you can create a simple one-pager that will act as your cheat sheet. This will act as a personal guideline of what steps you need to take and when to take them.

EXERCISE #4: TAKE ACTIONABLE NOTES

There are countless resources for learning a new skill. The challenge here is you need a system for turning information into actionable steps. Otherwise, you'll spin your wheels in the research phase and never *do* anything with what you've learned. That's why it's important to use a note-taking method that focuses on getting results.

Here are a few steps you can do to take action-oriented notes:

1. **Choose the device you'll use to record notes (pen and paper, laptop/tablet, or an audio recorder).** Just remember that the pen-and-paper approach is the scientifically proven best method for helping people retain the largest amount of information.

2. **Use the Cornell Method to format the pages in your notebook.** Here, you'll divide each page into three sections that can be used to jot down notes and identify key points along the way.

3. **Review your notes after each learning session.** Here, you will identify important concepts, insert key words into the cues section, and then create a summary of the information at the bottom of each page.

4. **Turn your notes into a one-pager that will act as a cheat sheet and action guide that you can use to implement the key strategies for your skill.** This will act as a simple action plan to use whenever you're implementing a lengthy process

It doesn't matter if you self-educate with a video, book, podcast, in a classroom, or by talking to others—if you follow these four steps for your note-taking efforts, you will compress a lot of information in a short amount of time—*without* feeling overwhelmed.

Step #5: Create a Project Around the Skill

Mastering a skill can be extremely challenging. You're getting a lot of information all at once, so it's hard to know what's important. The result is you often feel confused about *where* to get started. That's why it helps to create a project for each skill, because it will help you make effective decisions about your daily tasks. In this step, I'll go over the process to turn what you've learned into an action plan.

A quick reminder: not every skill will require this step. If it's a repetition-based skill, then much of your time will be focused on deliberate practice instead of managing a series of tasks. So, if you feel like you don't need a project to get started, then feel free to skip ahead to Step #6.

WHY SHOULD YOU CREATE A SKILL-SPECIFIC PROJECT?

It often takes years to master a skill. Usually, this involves completing hundreds of small steps and working at them daily. This means you can't write down "master the skill" on your to-do list and expect to complete it. Instead, you need to turn the notes you've compiled into an action-oriented project list. Specifically, you'll create tasks that will be worked into your weekly routine.

For instance, here are a few items you can include on this list:

- A due date if there's a specific deadline involved—including milestones for time-sensitive tasks.
- Scheduled appointments, conversations, and events that happen on a certain day.

- Single actions broken down into tasks that take a maximum of a few hours to complete.

- Resources, tools, and websites to research at a later point.

- Quantifiable habits to complete every day (like "write for 30 minutes" or "walk for 15 minutes").

This project list will act as your central hub for everything related to the skill you'd like to master. It will grow organically as you learn new things, test a strategy, and gain more experience. It will also shrink as you complete those small but important microsteps. Done correctly, you'll find that this project list will become an invaluable companion you'll refer to throughout the day.

It's not hard to create a project list. In fact, you can get started in five minutes with two great tools that are completely free.

TODOIST AND EVERNOTE: A PERFECT MATCH!

While the Cornell note-taking method helps you never lose an important piece of information, it's no substitute for tools that can digitize all you've learned and are *also* accessible no matter where you go or what device you're using. The two tools I'm referring to are Todoist and Evernote. Each has a specific benefit, so let me give you a brief overview of both, and then we'll talk about how they can be used to assist your mastery of a skill.

Evernote a cross-platform tool that allows you to take notes, capture ideas, and organize this information into a file structure that's based on your personal needs. You can use Evernote to create simple, text-based notes; upload photos; record voice reminders; add videos; and clip specific webpages. Anything that can be digitized can be uploaded to Evernote.

There are two purposes for which I recommend Evernote:

1. **As a central location to capture any important idea or thought.** This can be a strategy you'd like to implement, a website to

bookmark, or a time marker for a multimedia file related to your next skill. Basically, whenever you come across a piece of information that's important for your long-term success, it should go into Evernote.

2. **For storing the notes you've compiled while learning.** This allows you archive everything you've learned while having the ability to search through it using key words. If you type your notes, they can be uploaded directly into Evernote. Or, if you prefer the handwritten note-taking method, you can use one of these six options to scan these notes into a fully digitized, searchable file. The main point here is Evernote can serve as a virtual backup for all the information you've compiled while researching a skill.

It's easy to get started with Evernote. My recommendation is to create a "notebook" for your skill and then add notes for each reminder or idea that pops into your head. This article on Evernote can walk you through the entire process.

Todoist is the perfect tool for creating and managing project lists. I prefer this app over others because it allows you to maintain multiple projects and store tasks for each one, while also creating simple daily lists that don't cause you to feel overwhelmed.

Like Evernote, Todoist isn't difficult to use. Simply create a project for your skill, add tasks for that project, and then schedule these items into your weekly routine. To get started, the Todoist blog provides a quick starter guide.

If you feel confused by either of these apps, I've created a simple video that walks you through each one. You can access these videos on **the free companion website.**

Ask Yourself: "What's My Next Step?"

Getting Things Done by David Allen is one of the most popular productivity books around. The reason this book is beloved by so many is that Allen provides a simple framework for overcoming procrastination and taking consistent action on all our important projects.

A key lesson from *Getting Things Done* is to ask one question whenever you work on a project: "What's my next step?"

Once you've identified this task, you can start working on it and make forward progress on an important area in your life.

At first glance, this might seem like simplistic advice, but I think it's brilliant because it removes the overwhelm that many people experience with a large project. Instead of worrying about a hundred tasks, all you need to do is focus on the next step. You can accomplish amazing things by chipping away at a project, completing item after item.

Example

For the real estate investing project, the first major goal was to purchase my first investment property. This required me to complete a series of actions, like:

- Create a strict list of requirements for this property (e.g., location, price, crime rate, vacancy rates, 1% rule, and target cash-on-cash return).
- Research conventional loan companies in locations where I'm looking to invest:
  - » Do a quick Google search for each business.
  - » Call each company, talk to the mortgage loan originator, and find requirements for pre-approval.
  - » Work with the loan officer during the pre-approval process.
- Apply with my favorite conventional loan company.

- Research top three turnkey real estate companies:
  - » Do a quick Google search for each business.
  - » Check Better Business Bureau records.
  - » Call the company and talk to a representative.
  - » Call previous customers and ask about their experiences.
  - » Ask questions about this company in the Bigger Pockets forum.
- Pick my preferred turnkey real estate company and notify the point of contact about what type of properties I'm interested in purchasing.
- Compare each potential rental property to my strict list of requirements.
  - » This will be a daily, 5- to 10-minute habit. (More on this in a bit.)
- Bid on the properties that I like.
- Purchase the property.

I'll admit this project list is *far* from perfect. In fact, I could probably break it down into smaller, more manageable tasks. But the reason I've included it here is to show how you can turn any skill-based project into a series of action steps.

Creating a project list for your skill is the best way to implement what you learn. As you consume content through a book, podcast, video, or by talking to experts, look for specific strategies that you can execute immediately, and then do the following:

- Create a task and add it to Todoist.
- Organize this item so it's completed in the right sequence (i.e., you should know the type of property you want *before* reviewing different turnkey options).
- Add a reminder in Evernote if you can't take immediate action on this information.

- Look at each task to see if it should be broken down into smaller steps (i.e., you can break down the research of a loan company into a series of smaller tasks).

Overall, I'm a fan of the approach outlined in *Getting Things Done* because it removes the temptation to rely on memory alone to complete tasks. In fact, with a good organizational system, you get everything out of your head and put it into a central location. And then, whenever you're working on this skill, you can pull out this list and ask yourself: "What's my next step?"

PRACTICE JUST-IN-TIME LEARNING

We've already discussed the concept of just-in-time learning, but I want to briefly mention it again because it directly relates to your ability to act on the information you're consuming.

Mastering a skill doesn't mean studying for a few weeks (or even months) and *then* implementing these lessons. Instead, it's better to identify your current challenge, learn all you can about how to master it, and then go do what you've learned.

This deliberate practice (which we'll discuss in the next step) will become your best self-educational opportunity because you get real-world feedback on what works for your personal situation. More importantly, this will increase your commitment to the skill because you're not just sitting on the sidelines consuming content.

Example

Using our real estate investing example, right now, my main concern is learning how to master the process of buying single-family homes. This means I'm singularly focused on learning every strategy related to this goal. It also means that I'm proactively *ignoring* any information related to wholesaling, flipping, or buying land or commercial real estate. Perhaps I *might* be interested in these topics in the future, but for now, I tune them out because the just-in-time learning rule forces me to focus on a singular goal.

FORM A SKILL-SPECIFIC HABIT

We've talked about the single tasks on your skill-specific project, but how do you manage those recurring, daily actions? The simple answer is you turn these tasks into a habit!

For instance, let's continue with the real estate investing project list discussed earlier. I need to complete most of these tasks just one time. But if you look at the task that says, "Compare each potential rental property to my strict list of requirements," then you'll see this is a recurring activity. So, instead of crossing off this task from the list, I need to turn it into a daily habit.

A quick way to turn information into action is to plan your daily activities. Once a week, sit down and schedule tasks for the next seven days (I prefer to do this on Sunday nights). In your calendar, block out a specific time each day for when you'll complete the habit(s) related to this skill.

The total amount of time you invest is up to you (and the skill you'd like to master). It could be 5, 10, 30, or even 60 minutes a day. What truly matters is that you treat this like sacred time that you'll never blow off. No excuses here—just do it!

Now, if you're someone who has trouble sticking to a new habit, then you should check out one of these three tools:

1. Todoist: A great feature of this app is that you can create a repeating task that shows up on your daily list. This means you can schedule a habit for a certain time each day, which generates a notification that's displayed on your phone. It'll be hard to skip this activity if you always see an annoying pop-up message.

2. Habitica: This app gamifies your habits, where each task represents a monster that must be "conquered." The more habits you complete, the further you'll progress in the game.

   I'll admit the premise of Habitica is a little cheesy, but it's perfect for the nerdy folks (like me) who enjoy earning points and accolades for sticking to a habit.

3. Coach.me provides a social community where you can support others who are building habits while getting support in return. It's a simple app that's not hard to use on a consistent basis.

There are numerous apps you can use to build a skill-specific habit. I recommend these three because they perfectly combine technology, ease of use, and positive reinforcement to help users create habits that stick. If you want to learn more about habit development, then check out the eight-step plan for building habits that's part of the companion site.

THE TWO-TASK DAILY RULE FOR SKILL MASTERY

Becoming a skill expert can seem like a daunting prospect, but it's completely doable if you're willing to commit to daily, consistent action.

As Bill Gates famously said, "Most people overestimate what they can do in one year and underestimate what they can do in ten years."

My point is that you're a busy person with many things to do. So, what I *don't* recommend is convincing yourself that it's necessary to master a skill in the next month. This will only lead to frustration and burnout when you don't see instant results. Instead, it's better to focus on daily effort and celebrate those small wins as you work your way through the process.

You can make this happen by doing two things every day:

1. **Complete a recurring task.** This can be a simple five-minute habit or it can be a lengthy session of deliberate practice where you focus on mastering a small component of your skill. Schedule

this into your calendar and do everything you can to complete it on a consistent basis.

2. **Complete one project task.** This could be a simple task, like calling someone on the phone, listening to a podcast, or reading a book. It could also be a lengthier task that requires a few hours of effort. The important thing here is to spend time each day chipping away at your project list and working your way toward mastery.

Example

Currently, I have a daily routine for working on my real estate investing project list:

- Listen to podcasts whenever I'm driving, exercising, or running errands.

- Spend five minutes shopping for potential investments on my preferred turnkey website.

- Pull one item from my project list and schedule it into my routine. The task that I choose depends on how much time I can devote to this project *that day*.

Sounds easy, right?

Well, I think you can apply this strategy to your skill. All you need to do is schedule tasks into your day and make the commitment to complete them—without fail!

EXERCISE #5: CREATE A PROJECT AROUND THE SKILL

You can turn what you've learned into a series of tasks by doing the following:

- **Create a skill-specific project folder for your skill.** Do this inside the Evernote and Todoist apps. Or buy a notebook you'll dedicate to this project that will always be with you.

- **Write down all the tasks that you need to complete.** Be sure to include due dates, one-time tasks, resources to check out, and any habits you need to build. If you get stuck with this project list, simply ask: "What's my next step?" Then schedule it into your calendar.

- **Jot down every new lesson learned, potential strategy, or aha moment that comes to mind.** Put all of them into a central location that you constantly monitor. This could be in Evernote or in a physical notebook. What you choose isn't relevant. The important thing is to . . . Write. Down. Everything.

- **Focus on just-in-time learning, where you focus on tasks that directly relate to your most current challenge.** Work on this area until it's fully completed, then move on to the next step.

- **Build a habit related to your skill.** You can use apps like Todoist, Habitica, or Coach.me to reinforce this action.

- **Use the two-task rule to work at this skill daily.** One task should be a regular habit and the other will be pulled from your project list.

If you have a willingness to carve out time to work on a skill *every* day, you'll slowly make that transition from novice to expert!

Step #6: Deliberately Practice Every Day

Think back to the introduction of this book. There, I talked about two types of skills you can master: repetition-based skills and knowledge-based skills. Each requires a different pathway and action plan. A knowledge-based skill can be mastered through self-education, creating a project list, and learning as you implement each new strategy. A repetition-based skill can be mastered by identifying the most important components and then working at them daily. This is called deliberate practice.

In this last step, we'll talk about deliberate practice. Specifically, I will show you how to break down a skill into its smallest component and work at it every day to achieve mastery.

WHAT IS DELIBERATE PRACTICE?

K. Anders Ericsson first wrote about deliberate practice in his paper "The Role of Deliberate Practice in the Acquisition of Expert Performance." Here is what Ericsson himself had to say about this concept:

> We agree that expert performance is qualitatively different from normal performance, and even that expert performers have characteristics and abilities that are qualitatively different from or at least outside the range of those of normal adults. However, we deny that these differences are immutable, that is, due to innate talent.
>
> Only a few exceptions, most notably height, are genetically prescribed. Instead, we argue that the differences between

expert performers and normal adults reflect a life-long period of deliberate effort to improve performance in a specific domain.

So, to summarize, expert performance does exist. But while people might seem superhuman with their results, they really aren't. Instead, their results are largely due to a lot of hard work in a very specific area.

The big lesson here is when you put in the time, effort, and dedication to become the best in a specific area, it's possible to master it. But you will need to practice your craft for many hours, and, more importantly, you *must practice the right way.*

As you've learned throughout *Novice to Expert*, a lack of talent isn't an excuse. What we often perceive as someone's "natural ability" often comes from hours of daily deliberate practice that makes their performance look easy.

You can deliberately practice by following the following eight-step process.

STEP #1: UNDERSTAND THE FUNDAMENTALS

The most important aspect of deliberate practice is to *understand the fundamentals of the specific skill.*

Every skill is comprised of a series of small actions that are built on one another. So instead of focusing on all of them at once, it's better to laser-target a tiny component and spend a few sessions mastering it before moving on to the next one.

On his blog, James Clear provides a simple rule of thumb for this concept:

> **Deliberate practice is when you work on a skill that requires one to three practice sessions to master.** If it takes longer than that, then you are working on something that is too complex.
>
> Once you master this tiny behavior, you can move on to practicing the next small task that will take 1 to 3 sessions to master.

Aubrey Daniels provides another example of how to master the fundamentals when learning a skill:

> There are a great many factors involved in skill acquisition. For a simple example, consider the activity of two basketball players practicing free throws for one hour. Player A shoots 200 practice shots, Player B shoots 50. The Player B retrieves his own shots, dribbles leisurely and takes several breaks to talk to friends. Player A has a colleague who retrieves the ball after each attempt. The colleague keeps a record of shots made. If the shot is missed the colleague records whether the miss was short, long, left or right, and the shooter reviews the results after every 10 minutes of practice. To characterize their hour of practice as equal would hardly be accurate. Assuming this is typical of their practice routine and they are equally skilled at the start, which would you predict would be the better shooter after only 100 hours of practice?

As you can see, it's not enough to just practice something. To achieve true mastery, you need to identify each key component, work at it until becomes second nature, and then keep repeating this process for every component. So, let's talk about how to do that next.

STEP #2: PRACTICE (AND MASTER) EACH MICROCOMPONENT

Every day, you need to spend time in deliberate practice. This means repeating this process over and over until it's mastered. To demonstrate this concept, let's talk about how you could master the important elements of baseball.

If you tune in to any Major League Baseball game, you will see ballplayers who make their jobs look easy. They smack home runs, field grounders, catch fly balls on the run, and execute accurate throws across the field—all with perfect ease.

Now, I imagine if you talked to one of the players about his "natural talent," he would probably describe the thousands of hours of drills he's had to complete to achieve this level of skill. A ballplayer doesn't reach the big leagues through natural talent alone. Instead, he must practice (and master) every microcomponent of baseball.

For instance, just to master fielding a ground ball, a ballplayer needs to practice his ball-handling skills in a variety of scenarios. This means he needs to complete drills like catching a:

- short hop infield hit;
- ball-in-hand ground ball;
- outside-the-glove hit; and
- ball on one knee.

These are just a few drills a baseball player needs to practice for a *single* aspect of the game. So instead of trying to do them all at once, a smart ballplayer knows it's better to work on one component, spend a few sessions mastering it, and then move on to the next one.

When it comes to *your* skill, it's best to break down the process into a series of microcomponents. Spend one to three days mastering it, and move on to the next only when you feel comfortable completing this action. Keep repeating this process until you've mastered each of these components.

STEP #3: GET IMMEDIATE FEEDBACK FROM AN EXPERT

In addition to practicing the right things, it's equally important to get feedback from others as often as possible. This advice is important because it helps you understand what you're doing correctly and what you're doing incorrectly. Remember, *perfect* practice makes perfect.

For instance, if you spend a whole day on a baseball-throwing drill, but you do it incorrectly, then you've only reinforced a bad habit. However, if you get immediate feedback on your technique, then you learn how to deliberately practice the correct technique.

The best way to get feedback is to work with a coach or mentor. This is someone who has achieved expert status, so it's worth paying for their time because it will skyrocket your success and help you avoid the rookie mistakes that many people make.

Another thing to consider is you're not bound by a geographical location to work with a coach or mentor. Nowadays, it's easy to find help online and get feedback through a Skype video session. Following are just a few resources you can use to find a potential coach.

Coach.me not only allows you to track habits but it also has a marketplace where you can get online coaching at a low cost. While the coaching is not as in-depth as a live one-on-one call, it's a good service if you have a limited budget. Often, a weekly check-in is all you'll need to stick with a skill.

Coach.me also offers free community support via an online forum and Q&A section, so if you really don't have the budget, you can get help without spending a dollar. But keep in mind that you often get what you pay for. It has been said that the most expensive advice is free advice, because you never know if the person is an actual expert on the topic.

Clarity.fm connects people with top industry experts who help with market research, give strategic advice, and teach people how to master specialized business skills. It's a pay-per-call service. You let them know what your topic or question is, and they find you an expert and schedule the call so you can get the support and accountability you need.

The benefit of Clarity.fm is you're billed on a per-minute basis, so you won't need to pay for an hour-long call if you only need answers to a few questions.

Finally, Clarity.fm is an excellent place to test different coaches and hire the best one on a full-time basis. My advice is to pay for an introductory call with three or four potential coaches, talk with each for 30 minutes, and then hire the person who provides the most insight during your meeting. You can usually tell within the first five minutes whether a person can provide actionable advice.

Accomplishment Coaching lets you search for coaches by specific criteria: education, experience, and area of focus. This makes it easy to find the right coach to meet your needs. The Accomplishment Coaching website has a powerful quote: "Who exactly seeks out coaching? Winners who want even more out of life!"

Life Coach offers different levels of personal coaching and support based on your budget constraints. It features a user-friendly search option so you can find the type of coaching you need, like online coaching or phone coaching.

This may seem overly simple, but it's easy to find a long list of qualified coaches by doing a Google search for terms such as "personal coaching" or "life coaching." The coaches found online usually offer a wide range of services, from a short phone call to get you started all the way up to weekly coaching calls.

You can also search for a coach based on specific goals. Use terms like "writing coach," "business coach," or "relationship coach" to find the right person. See too many results? Add a modifier related to your geographic area, such as "writing coach New York" or "relationship coach San Francisco." Coaching is a big industry, so if you're willing to do your research, it's not hard to find a qualified person who specializes in helping people achieve mastery of a skill.

STEP #4: EMBRACE YOUR MISTAKES

Your daily practice session is an important time. It's your opportunity to work at a skill and focus on mastering it. It's also an opportunity for you to make a lot of mistakes in a safe environment where nobody will know about it (besides your coach or mentor).

We have been taught that mistakes are bad things. But it's been my experience that mistakes are the only way to truly learn a valuable lesson. They provide feedback on what *doesn't* work for your skill development. As Thomas Edison once said, "I have not failed. I've just found ten thousand ways that won't work."

Embracing your mistakes can be a powerful concept when it's used with just-in-time learning. You can identify an important concept, try it on your own, make a bunch of mistakes, and eventually master it because you're not afraid to keep working at it.

For instance, let's say you'd like to learn a new programming language. The simplest way to master it is to identify one drill or challenge, play around with it for a few practice sessions, and make a lot of mistakes along the way. Repeat this process every day until you've mastered that component, then move on to the next one.

STEP #5: SLOW DOWN YOUR DELIBERATE PRACTICE

It's not enough to chunk down a skill and master each component. You also need to slow down your efforts and practice it at half-speed.

Many people feel frustrated after making a mistake, so they end up rushing the next repetition. A better method is to take a few seconds to gather your thoughts, figure out what you did incorrectly, and then go even slower on the next repetition. Don't rush your efforts here. Just keep your deliberate practice slow until you feel comfortable increasing the speed.

STEP #6: COMPLETE NUMEROUS REPETITIONS

In addition to slowing things down, you need to repeat this component until it becomes second nature. What you're trying to do here is create that long-term muscle memory where you don't *think* about the process—your body automatically does it.

Odds are you've probably mastered many skills through muscle memory. If you can drive a car, touch-type, or play an instrument, then you probably do them without a lot of brainpower. Your body automatically acts because it has performed this process countless times.

Furthermore, this repetition provides an opportunity to challenge yourself by increasing the difficulty of the component. You can do this in a few ways:

- Find someone who is slightly better than you and compete against them (e.g., if you're trying to improve your basketball game, have a free throw shooting contest).

- Combine two skills you've mastered (e.g., if you're learning baseball, practice catching a short hop infield hit and then throwing it to first base).

- Perform a skill in unexpected, adverse conditions (e.g., if you're working on your public speaking skills, practice what you'll do if your slides aren't working).

- Put yourself in a "high-stakes" environment (e.g., if you're learning a language, book a trip to a country where most people don't speak English and force yourself to converse only in the native language).

Remember, the value of these repetitions is that you can deliberately practice in an environment where it's okay to make mistakes. This will give you the best education for what needs to be improved. Plus, it will prepare you for the times when you must perform the skill because it *really* counts.

STEP #7: TAKE BREAKS DURING EACH PRACTICE SESSION

A recent study found it's important to take frequent breaks because they improve your productivity and creativity. This is especially true for deliberate practice because learning a new skill is mentally *and* physically exhausting. When you schedule breaks into your practice session, you'll get better results because you're giving 100% effort for each repetition.

Breaks are extremely important for skills that require memorization. There is a concept called the serial position effect that shows people tend to remember the first few items (the primacy) *and* the last few items (the recency) of a sequence. This means if you're doing a marathon session of memorization, you'll decrease the likelihood of remembering every item. On the other hand, if you chop up a session and take frequent breaks, you'll remember more items because you're increasing the number of starting and stopping points.

A strategy that I recommend is the Pomodoro Technique, in which you focus on a single task for 25 minutes, take a 5-minute break, and then begin another 25-minute block of time. This strategy can be grueling at times, but it also helps you stay laser-focused on a skill.

You should work diligently while the clock is ticking, and when the timer goes off, allow yourself a short break to stretch, walk outside, close your eyes, or do whatever it takes to rejuvenate yourself. Try not to use this time to check emails, make a long phone call, or do anything that will steal your productive time.

STEP #8: TRACK YOUR SUCCESS

If you want to skyrocket your success, then you should diligently track each single practice session. Not only does this keep you motivated as you celebrate those small wins but it will also help you identify those small challenges that you're experiencing. The simplest way to track your success is to use a goal-oriented journal, like The Freedom Journal.

The Freedom Journal was launched in 2016 by John Lee Dumas, a popular entrepreneur and podcaster. While it's completely optional to the learning process, I recommend it because it can help you focus on a single major goal (like learning a new skill) and working on it for the next 100 days. If what you're trying to learn is personally important, then The Freedom Journal can help you stay on track and make sure that you're not losing momentum along the way.

MORE ON DELIBERATE PRACTICE

Before we move on, I'd like emphasize the importance of using deliberate practice to master a repetition-based skill. When you break down a process into small components then drill each on a continuous basis, you develop the unconscious competence (i.e., muscle memory) that will make your actions seem effortless.

I think deliberate practice is a fascinating concept, so I recommend you learn more about it. If you're interested, I recommend three great resources to get started:

- *Talent Is Overrated* by Geoff Colvin
- *The Talent Code* by Daniel Coyle
- *Expert Enough* (blog) by Corbett Barr

EXERCISE #6: DELIBERATELY PRACTICE EVERY DAY

It's not enough to set aside time to work at a skill. Instead, you should chunk down the process into its smallest components and then work at mastering each one before moving on. You can do this by completing the following eight steps:

1. **Understand the fundamentals.** Practice just-in-time learning to identify the critical components, or get a recommendation (from a coach) for specific drills to focus on.

2. **Practice (and master) each microcomponent.** Your goal is to master each aspect of the skill in one to three sessions. If you can't master it during this time, then look for a way to further drill down the skill into a smaller component.

3. **Get immediate feedback from a skill expert.** If you can hire a coach, then this will be a worthwhile investment. Otherwise, find videos of someone demonstrating this skill and ask a friend to provide a critique based on what you see.

4. **Embrace your mistakes.** Don't be afraid to make a mistake during these sessions. Sure, it might not be fun to make errors, but just remember this is an important part of the learning process.

5. **Slow down your deliberate practice.** You don't need to rush through a skill to master it. In fact, it's better to go as slowly as possible to understand how it works and then increase your speed as you start to achieve mastery.

6. **Complete many repetitions.** Doing the same thing over and over will build the muscle memory that's an important part of turning a skill into an unconscious action. In addition, you should consider increasing the difficulty of these practice sessions, so you perform well no matter what comes up.

7. **Take breaks during your practice session.** You'll find it's easier to retain information and master a skill by breaking down a

session into smaller segments with quick breaks. I recommend the Pomodoro Technique, where you work for 25 minutes, rest for 5, and then work for another 25 minutes. Repeat this process as often as you need.

8. **Track your success.** Record your progress in a journal and be honest about any challenges you're experiencing. My suggestion is to use a tool like The Freedom Journal.

You have a choice at the start of every new day. Either you choose to waste it by practicing a skill without a clear plan, or you choose to break it down into small components and then master each one. If you follow this action plan for deliberate practice, you will maximize the results you get from each session.

MASTERY IS AN EVOLUTION

Before writing this book, I asked for feedback on the title from a variety of writers. And the one comment that came up a few times is how I should add an expected time result to make the book sound more enticing, like *Novice to Expert in 30 Days or Novice to Expert in 15 Minutes a Day.*

I resisted this advice for one major reason: some skills take *years*, not days, to master. I'm sure you can master the art of folding clothes in an afternoon, but it will take you a much, *much* longer to become an expert surfer.

Every skill has a distinct group of components that need to be mastered through deliberate practice. So, if you want to build a skill that has a few hundred components, then it's going to take a few hundred practice sessions to achieve expert status.

One question you might ask while reading this book is, "How long will it take to achieve mastery?"

This is hard to answer because your results depend on many variables:

- What is the skill you're trying to learn?
- How much spare time can you devote to this skill?
- Who is your coach or mentor?
- What resources are you using to self-educate?
- How long is each practice session?
- What is the quality of each practice session?
- How often do you receive useful feedback from a coach or mentor?

As you can see, there are many factors that will determine your success with a skill. So, before we move to the final section of this book, I want to remind you of one thing: mastery is an evolution.

There isn't a "magic pill" resource that can help you achieve instant results with minimal effort. Sure, you'll find the occasional shortcut, but if you want to get *really* good at one thing, you should be prepared to work at this skill on a regular basis.

In fact, I expect to spend many years learning the ropes of real estate investing before I'd be comfortable calling myself an expert. But I'm perfectly happy with basking in my novice status for a while because it means I'm learning a skill where every day provides an opportunity to try something new. Hopefully, you have the same mindset when it comes to the skill *you* are trying to build.

6 Habit-Learning Challenges (and How to Overcome Them)

It's one thing to *try* a new skill, but it's a whole other thing to try to incorporate that skill into your busy day that's full of distractions. In fact, you probably deal with obstacles *all* the time. So, instead of quitting when things get rough, I encourage you to look for creative ways to overcome the various challenges you'll face.

In this section, I'll go over six challenges that people typically encounter whenever they try to add a new skill or habit into their day.

CHALLENGE #1: PROCRASTINATION OR DIFFICULTY GETTING STARTED

Many people put off getting started for a variety of reasons:

- They feel like they need more information before taking action.
- They are confused about what they need to do first.
- They have a fear of making mistakes.
- They feel overwhelmed by other life obligations.
- They make the process sound more difficult than it is.

It doesn't matter *why* you procrastinate. What's important is to recognize that you're making excuses, and then *do something* about it. So, here are three ways you can overcome this challenge and get started today:

1. Define the Individual Components of the Skill

A common reason people procrastinate is they're confused about where to get started. They'll create a goal (like "improve my credit score") but feel overwhelmed because it's a large task without any clearly definable actions. You can overcome this challenge by creating a project list (as described in Step #5) and defining each step of the process.

If you find that you're *really* struggling with procrastination, I recommend getting as granular as possible. This means identifying the smallest possible steps you need to take and scheduling them into your day.

For instance, if you would like to improve your credit score, the first seven items on your project list would look like this:

1. Research information on how to understand a credit report.
2. Go to Google and get the phone numbers of all three credit reporting agencies.
3. Call Experian to request your credit report.
4. Call Equifax to request your credit report.
5. Call TransUnion to request your credit report.
6. Go through each credit report and verify the accuracy of every item.
7. Submit disputes in writing for any inaccurate information to each credit report agency.

These are just a few items you can include in a project list. But don't they seem more doable than working on an ambiguous goal like "improve my credit score"? I think it's hard to procrastinate when you have a clear list of steps to follow that only take a few minutes of effort every day.

So, if you have difficulty with getting started, take ten minutes to write down the first steps of the process and then schedule time into your day where you can cross off at least one of these items from your list.

2. Get an Accountability Partner

People often procrastinate when it's too easy to not get started. If you're the only one who cares about this goal, then it's not hard to let yourself off the hook whenever you feel overwhelmed. That's why you should work with an accountability partner to create enough external motivation where you'll act—even when you don't feel like it.

An accountability partner is someone who takes personal responsibility for your commitment to a new goal. This could be a person you meet with on a regular basis or it could be an informal arrangement where you agree to support one another.

Any of the following people can be an accountability partner:

- Friend
- Family member
- Someone who shares a mutual interest in this skill
- Coach or mentor
- Member of an online forum or Facebook group
- Member of a local Meetup group

Really, the only two requirements you'll need for an accountability partner is they need to correspond with you on a regular basis and be willing to "call you out" whenever you procrastinate.

Accountability is an in-depth topic. If you want to learn more about it, then I recommend checking out my other book, *The Accountability Manifesto*.

3. Use If-Then Statements to Overcome Laziness

If-then statements can help you stick with a goal, and, more importantly, will prevent those times when you want to skip a day. The idea here is to identify your personal weaknesses, then create a plan for what you'll do when they occur. Whenever you feel like taking a day off, you'll follow this script and push yourself to get started.

To explain the if-then concept, let's talk about a study that psychologist Peter Gollwitzer completed in the mid-'90s.

In one experiment, Gollwitzer asked his students to mail in an assignment two days before Christmas. One group was given the assignment with no additional instructions, while the other was asked to form specific if-then statements: *when* they would mail it, *where* they would mail it, and *how* they would mail it.

The results were as follows:

- The first group (who had no specific instructions) had a 32% success rate.
- The second group (who had if-then instructions) had a 72% success rate.

By taking the time to create a plan, the people in the second group more than doubled their success rate.

Gollwitzer proved that the if-then group members were better able to follow through with their goals because they created a specific script of how they'd complete the goal while also identifying any obstacles along the way that might impede their chances of success.

The students involved in Gollwitzer's experiment recognized the potential pitfalls associated with the project: being too busy with other assignments, getting sidetracked by outside distractions, or even pure laziness. By forming if-then statements, the students clearly identified what *might* prevent them from completing the assignment and then adjusted accordingly.

Consider another example of using if-then statements to make sure you consistently work on your chosen skill.

Let's assume your goal is to master your financial literacy—specifically, you want to start by getting better at saving your money.

When it comes to a nebulous goal like "save more money," you would benefit by identifying the triggers that cause you to overspend and creating a series of if-then plans to overcome them.

You could do this in a few ways:

- "If I go to the mall, then I will avoid the shoe store."
- "If I end up in the shoe store, then I will not buy anything."
- "If I go to Amazon, then I will buy only things I need."
- "If I go out dancing, then I will avoid buying expensive drinks."
- "If I go shopping for Christmas presents, then I will stick to a budget."

To overcome procrastination, take a few minutes and think of all the excuses you say to yourself whenever you fail to work on a goal. Write down each one on a piece of paper. Then create an if-then plan for what you'll do if one of these challenges comes up. This will give you a clear set of instructions for how to act whenever you feel that mental impulse to skip a day.

CHALLENGE #2: FINDING THE TIME

Sometimes you feel like you're too busy to squeeze in time to work on a skill. This can be especially true if you schedule it in the evening, after you've already had a busy, stressful day. I'm not going to lie and say it's always easy to carve out a spare 30 minutes for a new goal, but there are three strategies you can use to "find" more time.

1. Say No to Certain Activities

Right now, there are probably a few activities that can be streamlined or even eliminated from your schedule. Perhaps you could skip a half hour of TV time. Or find a creative way to skip that low-value meeting that isn't important for your job. Or maybe you could bring a bag lunch to work, eat at your desk, and work on your skill during your lunch break.

My point is simple: you probably waste more time than you think. The obvious culprit is media consumption. It has been reported that the average US citizen spends eight hours consuming media: including watching television surfing the Internet. Even if you do both activities at the same time, that's still almost a *quarter* of your day spent on a pointless activity. If you can sacrifice just an hour of this time every day, that's one more hour than most people spend on their goals.

2. Maximize Those Small Pockets of Time

You'd be surprised at how much time you really have each day. The problem is, we've developed this mind-set in our culture that you need huge blocks of uninterrupted time to work on important tasks. But if you closely look at your daily routine, you'll see there are lots of 5- to 10-minute blocks of free time that can be leveraged.

Think of all the time you waste every day doing nothing: waiting in line at the store; sitting through commercial breaks; doing chores around the house; driving (or sitting in a bus) during your daily commute.

Most people spend this time playing games on their phones, checking their Facebook feeds, or reading the headline news. You, on the other hand, were smart enough to read this book, so you can take full benefit of this wasted time by working on your skill.

There are many activities you can do to progress your skill development during these small pockets of wasted time:

- Read an article, blog post, or part of a book.
- Listen to an audiobook or podcast.
- Make an important call that's related to a task on your project.
- Have a brief conversation with your accountability partner.
- Go through your project list and identify a few key steps.
- Review your notes and refresh your memory.
- Quiz yourself using physical flash cards or flash card software.

Sure, you might not have time for a full deliberate-practice session, but if you can do any of the above, then you'll maximize the time that other people typically waste.

3. Wake Up Earlier

If you want to learn something bad enough, then it's worth getting up earlier in the morning to work on this skill when distractions won't interrupt you. Now, this doesn't even mean you must lose sleep. In fact, if you go to bed 30 minutes earlier at night (maybe by skipping one TV show), then you'll feel just as rested when you get up in the morning.

Just do the math…30 minutes each day is an extra 210 minutes (or 3 hours 40 minutes) each week. Over a year's time, that's 182.5 hours that can be dedicated to deliberate practice. I guarantee this small change will give you enough time to have an amazing impact.

CHALLENGE #3: STICKING WITH A SKILL

In preparation for this book, I talked to many people who wanted to increase their success rates with skill development. One of the biggest complaints I heard from these folks is they would often start a new goal with a feeling of excitement but then quit a few weeks later because they couldn't stick with it.

One person had a great name for the failure to stick with a goal. He called it the "Valley of Despair." He described how it's easy for him to start a new project with a feeling of excitement, but this emotion quickly evaporates whenever he experiences any setback or challenge.

This Valley of Despair is a real thing that happens to anyone starting a new project. You start with happiness and excitement, but then you transition into fear, guilt, or even depression whenever something doesn't go according to plan.

Fortunately, there is a very powerful technique that I use whenever I'm starting something new and need to make it part of my daily routine. It works perfectly for those times when I want to skip a day. Let's talk about this technique.

Mini Habits: The Key to Sticking With a New Skill

Mini habits is a powerful concept that has revolutionized my ability to get things done without feeling like I'm missing anything important. This is a term coined by my friend Stephen Guise that helps people overcome their natural impulse to avoid difficult tasks.

The idea behind mini habits is to avoid those overly ambitious goals that people often set. When you consistently fail, it's easy to lose emotional momentum and then fall into the Valley of Despair. Stephen's point is that it's *not* the habit that causes you to fail. Instead, it's the *expectation* that you place on *how much* or *how long* you will do the habit.

As an example, let's say you set a goal to practice speaking Spanish for 90 minutes every day. You're able to do it for a few days, but then one day you need to stay late at work, and you go to bed exhausted. You skip the next day of practice because you're simply too tired to spend an hour and a half on this skill. This pattern continues for the next few weeks as you practice Spanish on one day but then skip it the next day. Finally, you give up on the habit because you simply can't stay consistent with your language lessons every day.

Stinks, doesn't it?

Fortunately, you can prevent this discouraging cycle by adopting the mini habits strategy. The idea here is to focus on *consistency* instead of a specific goal. All that matters is putting in *some* time on a daily basis.

The mini habits technique works because it prevents those feelings of overwhelm that happen when you set a goal that is too difficult to do every day. Guise explains, "When people try to change, they usually try to get amped up for the change, but no matter how badly you want the change, you haven't changed yet! As motivation wanes, so does progress. You don't need more motivation; you need a strategy that can leverage the abilities of the current you into a better you."

In other words, the simplest way to create a lasting change is to set a goal that is easy to complete on a consistent basis. So rather than committing hours of your time each day, it's better to create an initial goal (for *at least* a few weeks) where you only focus on this skill for 5 to 10 minutes a day. Obviously, you should *try* to do more, but aim for something that's doable no matter what comes up during the day.

There are five reasons why the mini habits concept can help you stick with a new skill:

1. **Your success will lead to more success.** It's easy to get discouraged when you fail repeatedly. On the other hand, a mini habit will create a sense of excitement because you're achieving an important daily goal. Trust me—when you have a 30-day streak going, it's easier to feel that excitement to get started each day.

2. **You will avoid the guilt trip.** It's fun to have a streak of consecutive days where you work at something new. This is the exact opposite of what happens when you miss a day or two. There is nothing to be gained by setting an overly ambitious goal. All this does is create a negative attitude toward an activity that's supposed to be fun.

3. **You increase the desire to work on this skill.** It's easy to procrastinate when you know that every day you "must" spend *hours* on a task. In fact, you'll quickly learn to dread this activity. But by setting an achievable goal, you push past that inertia and get started because the goal seems completely doable.

4. **You'll do more than planned.** A strange thing happens once you overcome your initial inertia and get started. What usually happens is you convince yourself to keep going and do way more than you'd planned. You're using the power of self-deception to trick yourself into getting started. This creates enough momentum that you'll keep going long after you've passed the daily goal.

5. **You'll form a habit.** Consistency is more important for building habits than hitting a specific metric. At first, an external cue will trigger your routine, like an alarm on your phone. But eventually, you'll simply remember to work at your skill at a specific time each day. This is what happens when you build a positive habit into your life.

If you find that you're struggling with sticking to a skill—or even getting started—try to set a mini goal that you can work on, no matter what happens in your life.

CHALLENGE #4: INABILITY TO STAY CONSISTENT

Our interests change as we get older. What once seemed important might not be so important later in life. This means you might not have the time (or the dedication) to work at a skill that was once a major passion. When this happens, you run the risk of experiencing "skill atrophy," where you forget how to do certain things.

This challenge is particularly troubling for anyone building a new skill. Since you need to reinforce this information regularly, when you take time off, the gains you made will quickly diminish. On the other hand, the more you've mastered a concept, the *less* daily reinforcement you'll need. If you can't devote a lot of time to an old skill, you can use the following strategies to keep your edge without it taking up too much of your time:

- **Pick one or two of the top-rated (or your favorite) industry-specific podcasts and listen to every new episode.** These should keep you on top of new trends, current events, and important resources to check out.

- **Read content from your favorite blogs and forums.** The same principle applies here—find a handful of trusted sources, then *filter out* all the other noise in your industry. Your time is valuable, so you don't want to waste mental bandwidth on websites that fail to provide useful information.

- **Teach this concept to others.** As mentioned before, the ultimate path to mastering a skill is to teach it to others. This will crystalize your thought patterns because you must think carefully about what's worked in your life and what hasn't.

Teaching can take any form. You could teach at your local college, create an online course, write a book on the subject, answer questions in a forum, or host a podcast. Really, there are so many avenues nowadays for teaching a subject. All you need to do is find a platform that *you* prefer and then start sharing your knowledge with students.

- **Form a mastermind group.** Like an accountability partner, you can regularly meet with people in your industry to talk about your skill *or* go out and practice it. This is called a mastermind group, because you gather together people who are at an equal level of success. The power of a mastermind group is you tap into the knowledge and experience of folks who have walked a similar path. Whenever you encounter an obstacle, you can turn to this group and get help.

- **Leverage your local Meetup groups.** You can use Meetup.com to find potential accountability partners or mastermind groups. The only difference is you can do it in a live setting (like meeting at a Starbucks once a month) and talk about your goals and current projects.

You might have noticed that these suggestions involve relying on your network to get up-to-date information.

The reason is simple—when you have achieved a certain level of mastery with a skill, you don't need to consume information for hours every day. Instead, it's better to rely on a handful of people and websites as your trusted sources. These will act as your information filters—pay attention to only what *they* recommend.

This is how I manage my education with the self-publishing industry. Currently, I only do the following to stay on top of this business:

- Write every day.
- Manage specific book marketing campaigns.
- Listen to three podcasts per week.
- Scan and read the headlines in a handful of Facebook groups for 5–10 minutes each day.
- Interact with a handful of top-level nonfiction authors in a private mastermind group.

- Buy the occasional course that teaches an emerging strategy or tactic.

By proactively setting up these information filters, I'm able to identify important strategies *without* feeling overwhelmed by an avalanche of "stuff" to do. In fact, the preceding list only requires about two hours of effort each day. This frees up my time so I can focus on mastering a *new* skill—real estate investing.

CHALLENGE #5: FEAR OF MISSING OUT (FOMO)

Fear of missing out (FOMO) is a phenomenon that happens to the best of us. You start something new, then hear about a different exciting opportunity. Then, you feel like if you don't try that new thing, you'll miss out and regret it later. FOMO can be a major issue, because it can distract you from the progress you've made on a new skill.

I've seen lots of people succumb to FOMO when trying to build an Internet-based business. There are new "opportunities" all the time, so it's hard for some to stick with one thing because what they're working on doesn't seem as sexy or exciting as the latest business model that *everybody* is talking about.

If you feel like FOMO is preventing you from taking action, you can overcome it by clearly identifying your priorities.

FOMO is often a symptom of an unconscious desire (or fear) in your life. If you find another interest that seems more interesting than what you're currently doing, then maybe it's a sign your actions aren't aligned with your goals. This is the point when you should decide to fully commit to what you're doing *or* immediately cut it out of your life.

A great story to illustrate this point comes from the Live Your Legend site, where Scott Dinsmore shares a story about meeting a friend of Warren Buffett's pilot (whom he calls Steve).

In this conversation, Steve talked about how Buffett encouraged him to write down a list of 25 things he wanted to do over the next few years. After completing this list, Buffett told him to review this list and circle his top five priorities. These goals would be more important than anything else in Steve's life.

Next, Steve was encouraged to create an action plan for these five activities. Buffett encouraged him to write them down as actionable goals and then get started on them immediately.

Toward the end of this conversation, Buffett asked a simple question: "But what about these other 20 things on your list that you didn't circle? What is your plan for completing those?"

Steve's reply was probably what most of us would say: "Well, the top five are my primary focus, but the other twenty come in at a close second. They are still important, so I'll work on those intermittently as I see fit as I'm getting through my top five. They are not as urgent, but I still plan to give them dedicated effort."

Buffett's reply was surprising: "No. You've got it wrong, Steve. Everything you didn't circle just became your 'avoid at all costs' list. No matter what, these things get no attention from you until you've succeeded with your top five."

Great advice, right?

Especially since it comes from one of the wealthiest people in the world.

I think the lesson here is that even though we live in an amazing world full of opportunities, it's risky to try them all. If you often succumb to "shiny object syndrome," you take away precious time that could be spent working on something that's truly important to you.

My advice is simple—in fact, it matches the advice shared by Warren Buffett:

- Write down a list of 25 priorities that you want to accomplish in the next five years.
- Identify the top five that are important *right now*. (Hint: One of them should be a skill you'd like to develop.)

- Identify the other 20 that might be a distraction from your 5 priorities. Make a mental commitment to avoid these activities at all costs.

- If you discover a new opportunity, add it to a list of ideas that you maintain in Evernote or Todoist.

- Once a month (at a maximum), review this list and decide if you want to shift priorities. Also, analyze your list of 20 secondary priorities to see if you'd rather work on one of these instead of your current projects.

- If you absolutely feel like you must work on something new, then immediately cut out one of the five original priorities. This is important because you'll avoid working on an ever-growing list of goals. This will dilute your focus and prevent you from achieving mastery with any skill.

We *all* feel the occasional pull of FOMO. It's easy to feel excited about something new because it represents an opportunity that hasn't been tried before. But if you recognize that FOMO is a dangerous mind-set, you can stay focused on the important projects in your life.

CHALLENGE #6: NOT RECEIVING SUPPORT

The people in your life can have a direct impact on your ability to stick with a long-term commitment (like learning a new skill). Often, the wrong comment or critique from the people that surround you can cause you to second-guess your efforts or even want to give up.

These comments could be anything like:
- "You don't have the background to do it."
- "What if something goes wrong?"
- "You are already busy; does this mean you'll have less time to spend with me?"
- "You know you're not smart enough to do this, right?"
- "What if you fail?"

Feedback like this can be emotionally crippling—especially when it comes from someone you love.

So, what can you do when you hear comments like these from the people in your life?

Well, there are three strategies you can use to communicate the importance of sticking with this skill.

First, pay attention to concerns and address them. Often, you'll get feedback that seems negative but comes from legitimate concerns that your partner might be feeling. This happens all the time whenever one person is trying to make a significant change to their life that might have a negative impact on everyone.

The simplest way to address this issue is to have an open dialogue where you both talk about your concerns. Get started by asking your partner to talk about their fears. Assure your partner they can be honest here. Don't judge or try to argue with these viewpoints, because they are legitimate feelings this person is experiencing. What's important is to get as much information as possible.

Next, you should leverage your network (i.e., a mentor, coach, accountability partner, or Meetup group) to get answers for your partner's concerns. This will help when you have a second conversation in which you try to alleviate your partner's fears. Again, this isn't about setting up a confrontation. Instead, you're trying to show that you understand their needs and are willing to come up with a solution for how you'll handle them.

Example

When I approached my wife about the idea of real estate investing, she expressed many concerns. One of them was: What would happen if I rented a house to a tenant who didn't pay or damaged the property?

She had a valid concern because we live a state (New Jersey) that is very "tenant-friendly," which often means a person could refuse to pay for a few months, trash the place, and it would still take *months* to have them evicted. In fact, we both have friends who tried to be landlords in New Jersey and hated it because they had a nightmare experience with evicting bad tenants.

When my wife expressed this concern, I immediately reached out to my network and asked for their advice. Literally within five minutes, I learned that many investors only buy properties in landlord-friendly states, where you can quickly evict bad tenants if they don't pay or if they damage the property. After explaining this strategy to my wife, I alleviated her fears because she knew that I was identifying the worst-case scenarios ahead of time and building preventative measures into my plan.

Hopefully, this illustrates the importance of having an open dialogue with the people in your life. If a friend or loved one points out a critical flaw in your plan, then perhaps it's a sign that you need to do additional research and make sure that you're not missing an important consideration.

Second, look for signs of emotional abuse. I'll admit this first strategy can be depressing. It's surprisingly common for people to end up in a relationship where one partner belittles the other or puts down their aspirations for self-improvement. Typically, this person will use a combination of sarcasm, cutting words, or even insulting language to get their way.

You should *never* accept this type of behavior because it is a sign of what's called emotional abuse.

If you ever express a desire to do something new and your partner shoots down your suggestions, then you must confront this behavior and communicate your needs. Only then can you escape the trap of emotional abuse and start to achieve the things *you* want from life.

Now, emotional abuse is a concept that goes way beyond the scope of this book. But my friend Barrie Davenport frequently writes about this subject. If you feel like this is a problem you're experiencing in your relationship, then I recommend checking out Barrie's book *Emotional Abuse Breakthrough*.

Third, surround yourself with like-minded people. Honestly, it's okay if a friend or family member isn't on board with your plan to work on a new skill. In fact, I'm a firm believer that everyone should have their own "thing." Instead of requiring them to be on board, you should meet new people and surround yourself with folks who share a similar level of passion for this skill.

Jim Rohn once said, "You are the sum of the five people you surround yourself with."

Although this well-known quote has been featured in countless self-improvement books, there has never been a truer statement. The people around you often determine your level of success in life. This is true whether you want to make more money, lose a few pounds, or build a new skill.

Your inner circle either has a positive or negative impact on what you can accomplish.

Just think of your life as it stands today. What are your major problems? Is there anything you would like to change? Are you achieving your goals?

Think carefully about the answers to these questions.

Odds are your response greatly depends on the people you engage with on a regular basis. You need to take 100% responsibility for your life—but it's possible to predict your level of achievement by closely examining your personal network.

My advice is simple. If you find that you're not being encouraged to continue with a skill, then perhaps it's time to surround yourself with people who can give you that supportive environment.

Just refer to Step #3 and connect with folks who share a mutual passion. What you'll discover is that when you more spend time with people who *enjoy* a particular skill and less time with those who dwell in negativity, you'll feel energized and excited to stay committed to this goal.

EXERCISE #7: OVERCOME SIX HABIT-LEARNING CHALLENGES

There are six challenges you might face when learning something new. If you don't know *how* to overcome these obstacles, you risk derailing your efforts. That's why I recommend doing the following to overcome each challenge.

CHALLENGE #1: PROCRASTINATION OR DIFFICULTY GETTING STARTED

- Define the individual components of the skill and identify the smallest actions you need to take to make forward progress.
- Get an accountability partner that you can meet with on a regular basis and openly talk about your challenges.
- Use if-then statements that will help you take action—even when you feel like skipping a day.

CHALLENGE #2: FINDING THE TIME

- Say no to activities like television, pointless meetings, and any section of the day that you're wasting.
- Maximize those small 5- to 10-minute pockets of time by consuming information related to your skill and completing small tasks.
- Go to bed 30 minutes earlier and then wake up 30 minutes sooner in the morning. Use this time to work on your skill.

CHALLENGE #3: STICKING WITH A SKILL

- Use the mini habits concept to set small goals that you can achieve every day—even when you don't have more than a spare five minutes.

CHALLENGE #4: INABILITY TO STAY CONSISTENT

- Practice the skill whenever you can.
- Pick one or two of the top-rated (or your favorite) industry-specific podcasts and listen to every new episode.
- Read content from your favorite blogs and forums.
- Teach this concept to others.
- Form a mastermind group.
- Leverage your local Meetup groups.

CHALLENGE #5: FEAR OF MISSING OUT (FOMO)

- Identify your top five priorities. Focus your efforts on just these activities.
- Identify your next 20 priorities.
- Make sure that you avoid these 20 activities at all costs unless you're willing to replace one of your current top five priorities with one of the 20.

CHALLENGE #6: NOT RECEIVING SUPPORT

- Pay attention to the concerns of the people in your life and address them by having an open dialogue about their fears.

  Look for signs of emotional abuse and confront this behavior from your significant other.

- Surround yourself with like-minded people who will support your efforts to work on this skill.

Final Thoughts on *Novice to Expert*

Tony Robbins often says that "success leaves clues." His point is that no matter what you want to learn, somebody, somewhere has already accomplished that goal. All you need to do is follow *their* path to increase your chances of achieving a similar level of success.

I feel this advice is especially true if you'd like to build a new skill.

We currently live in an amazing age where you can learn anything with just a few clicks of the mouse. And if you can't find the answer online? Then you can leverage the power of the Internet to meet local experts who can help you.

Nowadays, it's not hard to achieve expertise, because there is an abundance of information you can use to overcome any obstacle. Sometimes it'll take a few weeks to achieve mastery. Other times, you might need to work at it for years before experiencing a breakthrough. The important thing to understand is that you *can* learn anything if you're willing to work at it daily.

All you need to do is follow the six-step process that I outlined throughout this book:

1. Identify your preferred learning style.
2. Pick a single skill that you'd like to master.
3. Build the learning habit and surround yourself with quality information.
4. Take action-oriented notes.
5. Create a project around this skill.
6. Deliberately practice this skill every day.

There's your six-step plan for tackling any skill and working at it on a consistent basis. If you stay committed to this path, you can transition from a novice to an expert.

Now it's time to take what you've learned and implement this information. I guarantee that if you work at one skill every day, you'll be on the road to mastery in no time.

I'd wish you good luck to close out this book, but by now, I think you know that you're in charge of your own luck. Instead, I'll simply say . . .

Go forth and conquer!

Steve "S.J." Scott

One Last Reminder...

We've covered a wealth of information in this book, but that doesn't mean your self-educational efforts should end here. In fact, I've created a small companion website that includes many resources mentioned throughout *Novice To Expert*.

Here are just a few things I've included

- All the exercises in one downloadable file
- *147 Websites and Apps to Learn Something New* (a 9,000 Word Report)
- The Evernote walkthrough video
- The Todoist walkthrough video
- How to optimize Stitcher walkthrough video
- The one-pager example of my self-publishing process (PDF)
- *8 Steps for Building a Habit* (a short report)

Plus, I will be adding more goodies to this website in the months to come. So, if you're interested in expanding on what you've learned in this book, then click this link and join us today: www.developgoodhabits.com/expertwebsite

Thank You

Before you go, I'd like to say "thank you" for purchasing my guide.

I know you could have picked from dozens of books on habit development, but you took a chance with my system.

So a big thanks for downloading this book and reading all the way to the end.

Now I'd like ask for a *small* favor. Could you please take a minute or two and leave a review for this book on Amazon?

This feedback will help me continue to write the kind of Kindle books that help you get results. And if you loved it, then please let me know :-)

More Books by Steve

Declutter Your Mind: How to Stop Worrying, Relieve Anxiety, and Eliminate Negative Thinking

The Miracle Morning for Writers: How to Build a Writing Ritual That Increases Your Impact and Your Income

10-Minute Digital Declutter: The Simple Habit to Eliminate Technology Overload

10-Minute Declutter: The Stress-Free Habit for Simplifying Your Home

The Accountability Manifesto: How Accountability Helps You Stick to Goals

Confident You: An Introvert's Guide to Success in Life and Business

Exercise Every Day: 32 Tactics for Building the Exercise Habit (Even If You Hate Working Out)

The Daily Entrepreneur: 33 Success Habits for Small Business Owners, Freelancers and Aspiring 9-to-5 Escape Artists

Master Evernote: The Unofficial Guide to Organizing Your Life with Evernote (Plus 75 Ideas for Getting Started)

Bad Habits No More: 25 Steps to Break Any Bad Habit

Habit Stacking: 97 Small Life Changes That Take Five Minutes or Less

To-Do List Makeover: A Simple Guide to Getting the Important Things Done

23 Anti-Procrastination Habits: How to Stop Being Lazy and Get Results in Your Life

S.M.A.R.T. Goals Made Simple: 10 Steps to Master Your Personal and Career Goals

115 Productivity Apps to Maximize Your Time: Apps for iPhone, iPad, Android, Kindle Fire and PC/iOS Desktop Computers

Writing Habit Mastery: How to Write 2,000 Words a Day and Forever Cure Writer's Block

Declutter Your Inbox: 9 Proven Steps to Eliminate Email Overload

Wake Up Successful: How to Increase Your Energy and Achieve Any Goal with a Morning Routine

10,000 Steps Blueprint: The Daily Walking Habit for Healthy Weight Loss and Lifelong Fitness

70 Healthy Habits: How to Eat Better, Feel Great, Get More Energy and Live a Healthy Lifestyle

Resolutions That Stick! How 12 Habits Can Transform Your New Year

All of Steve's books can be found at: www.developgoodhabits.com

About the Author

In his books, S.J. Scott provides daily action plans for every area of your life: health, fitness, work and personal relationships. Unlike other personal development guides, his content focuses on taking action. So instead of reading over-hyped strategies that rarely work in the real-world, you'll get information that can be immediately implemented.

Made in the USA
Lexington, KY
16 January 2017